The Road to Santiago

KATHRYN HARRISON

The Road to Santiago

NATIONAL GEOGRAPHIC DIRECTIONS

NATIONAL GEOGRAPHIC
Washington, D.C.

Published by the National Geographic Society
1145 17th Street, N.W., Washington, DC 20036-4688

Text copyright © 2003 Kathryn Harrison
Map copyright © 2003 National Geographic Society

Library of Congress Cataloging-in-Publication Data

Harrison, Kathryn
    The road to Santiago / Kathryn Harrison
        p. cm. -- (National Geographic directions)
    ISBN: 0-7922-3745-5 (hc.)
        1. Spain, Northern--Description and travel. 2. Christian pilgrims and pilgrimages--Spain--Santiago de Compostela. 3. Harrison, Kathryn--Travel--Spain, Northern. 4. Santiago de Compostela (Spain) I. Title. II. Series.

DP285.H37 2003
818'.5403--dc21

                                                    200305438

Interior design by Michael Ian Kaye and Tuan Ching, Ogilvy & Mather, Brand Integration Group

Printed in the U.S.A.

For Jean

CONTENTS

The Road to Santiago

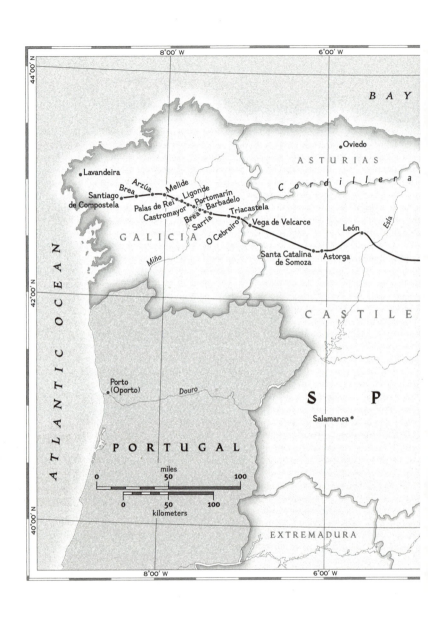

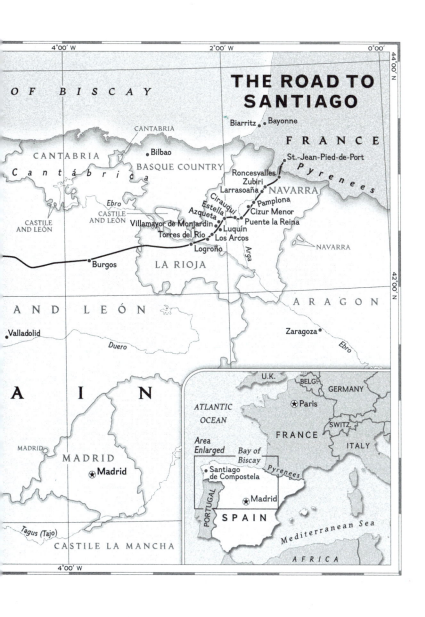

THE ROAD TO SANTIAGO

GULF OF BISCAY

OF BISCAY

CANTABRIA

Bilbao

CANTABRIA

C a n t á b r i c a

CASTILE AND LEÓN

Ebro

CASTILE AND LEÓN

BASQUE COUNTRY

Biarritz • Bayonne

FRANCE

St.-Jean-Pied-de-Port

Pyrenees

Roncesvalles
Zubiri
Larrasoaña

NAVARRA

Pamplona

Cirauqui
Estella
Azqueta
Villamayor de Monjardin
Torres del Río
Luquín
Los Arcos
Logroño

Cizur Menor
Puente la Reina

Burgos

LA RIOJA

Arga

NAVARRA

AND LEÓN

Valladolid

Duero

ARAGON

Zaragoza

Ebro

AIN

MADRID

MADRID

Madrid

Tagus (Tajo)

CASTILE LA MANCHA

U.K.

ATLANTIC OCEAN

Area Enlarged

Santiago de Compostela

PORTUGAL

SPAIN

BELG.

Paris

FRANCE

GERMANY

SWITZ.

ITALY

Bay of Biscay

Pyrenees

Madrid

Mediterranean Sea

AFRICA

PART ONE: 2002

One

Tuesday, July 23, 2002. 7:30 a.m. Paris.
Wan morning light. My daughter and I have just arrived
at Charles de Gaulle Airport on the night flight from
New York City. A sign tells us we're in Terminal C; our
tickets say our connection to Biarritz departs from
Terminal F. Two movies, two meals, magazines and
chocolate and a scant hour or so of sleep—and still Sarah
runs against the flow of an automated walkway. Twelve
years old, oblivious to the clots of weary crumpled pas-
sengers as they are passively transported from one
discomfort to another, blind to the man who watches
her long tanned legs just a beat too long, dismissive of
airport personnel who broadcast warning frowns, she

waves and smiles at me from under her lurching pack. *"Non, non!"* a woman in a uniform cries, pointing a finger at me, the delinquent mother standing where the ground doesn't shift, between two long people movers, but I don't stop my renegade child. Having timed it perfectly, Sarah is mesmerizing, running toward me in slow motion, just exactly as fast as the walkway tries to carry her away. Sneakers and shorts, unbound dark hair, blue eyes that startle with their size and intensity: a sprite delivering a message. Or is she asking a question: What are we doing here? Why have we come?

I step onto the sliding black rubber, and she turns around and takes her place beside me. Having missed a night's rest, I've lost the psychic insulation that protected me just yesterday from the quixotic nature of this trip, one revealed by the gray light of a Paris workday as a romantic absurdity. I'm employing twenty-first-century speed to transport the two of us, as quickly as possible and sleep be damned, to a tiny town in the Pyrenees from which we will begin a journey unaided by even the wheel. From St.-Jean-Pied-de-Port, in France, over the mountains to Roncesvalles, in Spain, and on to Pamplona, perhaps even as far as Logroño, we'll walk west carrying what we need. In a week we'll cover as much as we can of the ancient pilgrim road to Santiago de Compostela.

The road was established during the Crusades, those who walked it impelled by the same motive that lured others to the Holy Land: Here was a means of declaring allegiance to their God. Like all such voyages, the destination of Santiago offered less spiritual reward than the journey itself, which was a protracted penance, a great act of faith composed of many smaller moments of faith, at whose end lay the relics of a martyr—if, in fact, St. James is buried in Spain, because from the beginning of his story desire pushed truth toward romance.

The Gospels tell us that James, son of Zebedee, was in his boat mending his nets with his brother, John, when Christ summoned them, saying, "Follow me and I will make you fishers of men." James and his brother did follow, and James saw when Christ raised Jairus's daughter from the dead; he witnessed Jesus's transfiguration on the Mount, a new order of love supplanting the old of law; and he accompanied his Lord from glory to agony. James was with Christ at Gethsemane, and he asked to share in Christ's passion, asked for what he could not in his mortality anticipate, to be persecuted, and murdered, for his faith. In A.D. 44, James was beheaded in Jerusalem by Herod. As he had been the most zealous and aggressive of the Apostles, so was he the first to be martyred, and the first around whom legends collected.

Kneeling as he died, James caught his head in his arms and held it tight. Disciples took his corpse and placed it just so, arms still cradling head, in a marble sarcophagus, which they carried to Spain in a rudderless stone boat. The miraculous journey across the Mediterranean and through the Strait of Gibraltar took seven days—seven, like forty, being a charged and mystical number: the time it takes to make, or unmake, history. As the boat approached the shore it was greeted by a bridegroom riding a horse, neatly joining an image of Christ with that of the sea god Poseidon, who sometimes takes the form of a horse or bull. Impatient, the animal plunged into the water and emerged covered with white scallop shells, and so James was given his symbol, borrowed perhaps from Aphrodite, goddess of love.

A suitable burial place lay, however, on the other side of a thicket of trials. The pagan queen Lupa is said to have directed the disciples up a mountain where she expected they would be trampled by wild bulls or, failing that, devoured by a local dragon. But the sign of the cross transformed the bulls into docile guides, who returned the disciples and the saint's relics to the wicked queen. In the way of fairy tales, Lupa was immediately vanquished by the miracle and became a Christian. She made her palace into St. James's—or, to use the Spanish, Santiago's—first church and arranged for the marble sarcophagus to be hidden in a cave, where it remained undisturbed for eight centuries.

A rudderless stone boat crosses rough seas in seven days. Ridiculous. So why does the legend persist, told and retold through the centuries? Why do we cling to it unreasonably, as the saint did his severed head? During a holy year, when St. James's day, July 25, falls on a Sunday, over one hundred thousand people, children of the twenty-first century, walk the road to Santiago. So even now—when overnight we can exchange one life for another, put aside work to watch movies in midair, fly ahead of the Earth's turning, conspire with time, collapse the night, hurry the morning, speak across continents through cables bearing light—even now, we walk, making slow progress toward the invisible, the improbable, the ridiculous. No matter our faith, or lack thereof, we must travel away from reason to reach a state we hold in greater esteem: enlightenment.

Sarah and I step off the moving walkway; the linoleum floor jolts our feet. We walk the rest of the way to Terminal F unassisted by technology. Among the promises of Santiago is an altered relationship with time, the attempt to measure it step by step. Not to defeat time, nor to fight against its relentlessness, but to perceive time, one of the faces of God—a face routinely obscured by our modern multitasking lives.

In the ninth century, after the invasion of Spain by the Moors, St. James appeared, to some as a vision, to others as an idea: Could he offer a means of resisting the rising tide of infidels? One night a band of Christian hermits, among them a man named Pelayo, who had settled in Galicia (then called Asturias), saw lights in a forest, a *compostela* or field of stars. The apparition was accompanied by celestial music, and Pelayo followed the lights and the singing to find an altar raised on a marble sarcophagus and inscribed, "Here lies Santiago, son of Zebedee and Salome, brother of St. John, whom Herod beheaded in Jerusalem." Pelayo went to his bishop, Teodomiro, who confirmed the auspicious discovery and relayed it to King Alfonso. Now Christian Spain had the means to create a great shrine that might compete with Muslim Córdoba. The relics were moved and a new holy city, Santiago de Compostela, was born. Routes were established from France, from Italy, from Germany, most converging at a point in the Pyrenees, near the mountain pass of Cize. All were blighted by bandits, fraudulent priests, hawkers of indulgences, and horse thieves; such parasites abounded; genuinely Good Samaritans were rare. A twelfth-century French monk, Aymeric Picaud, compiled the first practical guide to the Camino de Santiago, a work that has been recapitulated many times and that is quoted in the literature I carry as I set off with my daughter.

The guidebooks are not light, but a heap of magazines and cheap paperbacks from the airport stores has made our backpacks pounds heavier. Walking through the airport's punishingly long corridors I realize, as I haven't before, that for this ascetic exercise I've chosen as my companion an adolescent girl, a creature defined by her enthusiasm for acquiring the very things I am trying to leave behind: CDs, magazines, accessories, cosmetics. With the added amusements, the packs barely fit into the connecting flight's overhead bins.

In Biarritz, I consult with the woman at the tourist information desk, suffering the humiliations of my rusty French, buying unnecessary maps from the stall next door to help me understand her suggestions. From the local airport we must take a bus to Bayonne, and from Bayonne a train to St.-Jean-Pied-de-Port. Finally, we are beginning to slow down. In Bayonne, we have an hour and a half to wait before our train's departure and spend it looking for trousers for Sarah, who hasn't packed a single pair of long pants, and whose mother was so flattened by the humidity of July in New York, and so apprehensive of the summer heat of Spain, that she forgot what lay in between—the Pyrenees. Bayonne is cold and wet. Rain slants across the mud-colored Nive River as we walk back over the bridge that separates us from the shopping district, where in one of the many ill-stocked shops we at last find a pair of serviceable wine-colored corduroys.

Back in the train station, Sarah discovers a photo booth that produces astonishingly beautiful pictures, as impossibly beautiful as an enchantment, and only two euros for one large, four small, or sixteen tiny prints. We fill the remaining minutes by reproducing her, and I study the shots as they emerge from the slot. Sarah is lovely anyway, lovely with braces on her teeth, lovely with unbrushed hair, eyes shadowed with fatigue, but something—what? the stark white backdrop? the digital camera? the strobe of the flash?—has produced mechanical alchemy. Each image glows like an icon.

"You try it," she says, but I don't want to break the spell.

"Here," I say, "don't let them get scratched." I hold open a guidebook, and we tuck them between its pages.

On the train to St.-Jean-Pied-de-Port, my daughter falls asleep, and I stare out the window trying to analyze the pleasure of European trains, whose hard third-class seats feel more luxurious to me than a Metroliner's plush recliners. It must be distance that affords such comfort. At home, I veer between responsibilities and deadlines, track ticking beneath the wheels, the noise of a vast clock. Here, the sound of the ties is soothing.

We disembark and walk into town, a pretty place, if we weren't too tired to notice. One hotel is full, and then another. It's nearly six o'clock, and I hope I haven't blown it—traveling with my child I can't afford the kind of miscalculations I've taught myself to take in stride. I walk up the steep sidewalk without looking at Sarah's face, avoiding what I might see there: disappointment, exhaustion, anxiety. A night on a bench is not an option, and, luckily, the fates agree. The next hotel has a sign with three stars, a restaurant, cable television, eiderdown duvets with white damask covers, and a vacancy.

I open our room's wood shutters, look out on quaint cobbles and window boxes filled with red geraniums, with a dramatic backdrop. "Look at the mountains!" I say.

"French MTV!" Sarah answers, ecstatic, waving the remote control. But we both fall asleep without taking off our shoes.

Wednesday, July 24, 2002. 7:30 a.m. St.-Jean-Pied-de-Port. Sarah sleeps while I jettison. This time, as with the first time I walked the pilgrim road, three years earlier, I am interested to discover what it is I discard en route, what

I thought I wanted enough to carry on my back but decide that, in fact, I don't. I sort through my toiletries and get rid of the extra soap and a leaking bottle of sunscreen. Having come with an abundance of maps and having bought more in the airport, I sacrifice three of the seven, and one of the guidebooks as well. The road is so well marked that a child, pre-literate, could follow the yellow arrows and red stripes across all of Spain, but I've forgotten this. I hold onto the security of maps and guides I don't need and won't use.

Traditionally, pilgrims carried a staff, both as support for the long, weary walk, and as a means of fending off dogs and thieves. They carried their water in gourds, and announced themselves as pilgrims bound for Santiago by displaying a scallop shell. All of these items, as well as their modern equivalents—graphite poles and canteens and Gortex jackets—are available in one after another store in the town of St.-Jean. After breakfast and a hot shower, we set out under our packs for the Accueil St. Jacques, the pilgrim office at 39, rue de la Citadelle, where we apply for our *credenciales*, or pilgrim records, which will enable us to use the *refugios* along the road, should we need them. The credencial, which costs a few euros, is meant to be stamped each day, at a refugio or a church or town hall; at the end of the road it can be presented at the Santiago pilgrim office for a certificate confirming the completion of the pilgrimage. What are the reasons for our undertaking the journey, the document demands. Catholic? Spiritual? Health? Other?

"What do I check?" Sarah asks me, and I shrug.

"Check what you want." She looks at my pen, hesitating between Catholic and Spiritual before I check both.

"*Are* you a Catholic?" she says. "Really a Catholic?"

"That would depend on whom you ask. The church has already decided that since Dad and I married in a Quaker Meeting, and since we never had any of you baptized, I am not. But inside, I think I am. At least I'm more Catholic than I am anything else."

She nods slowly. As she knows, before I joined my mother in a confirmation class and converted, at twelve, to Catholicism, I was raised by Jewish grandparents and thoroughly indoctrinated by ten years of Christian Science Sunday school.

"I'm leaving it blank," Sarah says.

"Fine."

More immediately concerned with our physical safety than with the state of our souls, the personnel in the pilgrim office protest that, given the forecast of rain and obliterating fog in the mountains, it is hours too late for us to begin walking today, when the road climbs and descends 1,250 meters through the Pyrenees, and offers no possibility of stopping after the Cize Pass.

"How far is it, exactly, to Roncesvalles?" I ask the woman on the other side of the desk.

"Twenty-seven kilometers. You must begin by seven. Eight at the very latest." She looks meaningfully at my daughter, telling me what I know, that my traveling companion is a child. Then she crosses her arms like a school marm, inspiring defiance. If we stay in St.-Jean, we'll be bored; we'll walk up and down the few streets, poke in and out of little shops; to kill time, inevitably we'll buy more things to carry; and the next day's weather may be no better.

"Thank you for your help," I say to the woman, and I stand and pick up my pack. "Thank you very much."

Outside the door, I look at the mountains, their peaks invisible in the clouds, and then at Sarah. "What do you think we should do?" I ask her. She scowls at the door to the pilgrim office.

"What a know-it-all. What a grump," she says. "Let's start. Let's go."

"I think so, too." We buy plastic ponchos and water and food—the packs are now very heavy—and set off. It is eleven, and I am anxious. Already I've done what I promised my husband I wouldn't: embarked on a day that will keep us walking too long and too late, walking into the dark hours. Already I've ceded decision-making power to a twelve-year-old.

On the other hand, she's a lot more practical than I am.

The road climbs steeply out of town, cleaving to an asphalt track and then diverging through pastures and groves of dripping trees. By all accounts, we miss some spectacular views as we ascend, and yet the fog provides a perfect transition into this life of walking. Luminous and swirling, dissolving the road behind and before us, it erases past and future. To break the unearthly silence, Sarah, who has just the previous week returned from summer camp, recounts a bunkmate's retelling of an episode of *The Twilight Zone*. In it, a man sets off on a road alone, encountering the same hitchhiker again and again, even though the driver keeps passing him in his car. Of course it turns out that the man in the car has died, driven into his afterlife without realizing he's left his old one behind. As I remember the series, it seems that a pet theme of *The Twilight Zone* was our mortal inability to acknowledge the death we hold within us. We walk, and I picture the black-and-white titles of the show, my grandfather's cracked leather chair, where I huddled under a blanket when I watched TV in his and my grandmother's gloomy, shabby den—a room that no longer exists, the house now gone, razed to build another home, the grandparents dead as well.

The road to Santiago heads west, relentlessly west, toward sunset and toward death. Centuries earlier, a pilgrim would sell all his possessions, divesting himself in anticipation of a journey he didn't necessarily expect to survive or complete. This time, my third experience of the road, I myself won't get as far as I plan on this first day of walking with my daughter. This particular journey, I'll discover, will be about discovering the grace to quit.

We've stopped talking, and the road has melted into nothing, when abruptly we arrive at the kind of vista I associate with dreams: all of life is spread at our feet, and where we are is cool and lovely and calm, villages and pastures seen from an astonishing height. Can we have walked all this way up? Did we, step by step, purchase this perspective, this shocking beauty? We let our packs slide off our backs, unfold one of the plastic ponchos to protect us from the wet grass where we sit to eat what we've bought in the town, a crusty baguette, a Dutch cheese sealed in red wax, pears, oranges, water. Beside a pilgrim's pump, from which we top off our water bottles, we see our first cairn.

"What is that?" Sarah asks.

"Just rocks. People add them, one by one, as they walk by."

"For what?"

"For whatever. Different reasons for different rocks, different pilgrims. You can, too, if you like."

Sarah regards the pile with her signature reserve. She doesn't hurry to join any crowd. "Maybe," she says, but she doesn't add one, and neither do I. Later she'll point out other heaps of rocks: "There's one," she'll say or, if it's an ambiguous, tumbledown pile, "Is that one?" Sometimes a cross made of twigs is tucked among the stones, and we stop to consider these, the bright yarn that binds the bits of wood together. We say nothing but I think we arrive separately at the same conclusion: The simplicity of the gesture is a quality neither of us possesses.

The one spectacular vista is the first and last we have, and in fact it disappears before our eyes, leaving us in the fog, not talking as we walk but listening to the eerie music made by bells hung around the necks of invisible goats and cows. Atonal, gonging out of the mist, abruptly near and then very distant, it underscores how solitary is our pursuit. Having been warned many times that July is the height of the pilgrim season, I'd anticipated—dreaded—crowds along the road, even imagining something like a slow motion marathon, but today we've seen no one.

"Surreal," Sarah says at last, and she's right.

The sun doesn't penetrate but illuminates the fog, thoroughly enough that we are walking through a weird, ambient cloud of light. Several times I try to identify the general direction of the sun but can't find any one area of the sky that is brighter than another. Still, we have enough visibility to find the trail markers—two red directional stripes painted on tree trunks, on stones, on any available surface, the occasional red "x" warning of a misstep—and to pick out the outlines of goats and sheep, the flowers underfoot, the grass and the trees. But there are the moments when we have to look, hard, for a marker, and then I remember the cautions of the pilgrim office back in town.

We come to a stone fountain on a hilltop, and a plaque, translated as: HERE ROLAND FELL. On either side is a vast army of tree trunks, frozen and alert, and then the ground drops away into mist. Sometime around A.D. 780, after a successful campaign to subdue the Saracens, Charlemagne returned to France with his foot soldiers. He had liberated Spain from the infidels, following the exhortations of three visions of St. James, who promised him divine assistance if he waged war on the Moors. St. James was as good as his word: the walls of Pamplona fell like those of Jericho, and other impossible victories followed. The vanquished Saracens provided the gold that financed the building of a great cathedral in Santiago. Alas, the subjugation of the Moors was neither complete nor permanent. Charlemagne's armies were ambushed in the Pyrenees, where Roland fell. There the king picked up and carried the body of the dead hero, his anguished cries echoing forward through the centuries, seeming, like the mournful bells of the animals we cannot see, to rush past me in the fog.

"Roland died in this place," I tell my daughter, huddled by the water fountain, shrouded in her dripping poncho. She nods. He is a name, no more than that, but the stone bearing his simple epitaph is pitted with age and conveys a heavy grief, enough to prophesy all our ends.

"Let's go," she says. "Let's keep walking."

The dripping dank weather, the steep climb, the unaccustomed weight of the pack, and the charm of the town we left behind—the hot breakfast we had so many hours ago—all of these encourage our fantasies of the place we are approaching. What will materialize at the end of today's twenty-seven kilometers? Heading downhill now, we pause at a signpost. Two routes will bring us to Roncesvalles: The shorter one, about three and a half kilometers, cuts through a beech wood; the longer, six kilometers, will take us through pastureland.

Sarah lets her pack slide off and sits while I consult various guides: the books I brought from home as well as the more detailed photocopies we were given in the pilgrim office, maps that tempt me to choose the wooded trail, to follow that straight line rather than the winding, less efficient route through open country.

It's six o'clock; we've depleted our provisions and our water; the fog is no longer white but gray and darker gray; the trees drip ominously. In my head I replay the conversation I had with my husband, a less reckless soul than I, the one about how fatigue leads to bad decisions.

"Don't you think," I ask Sarah, "that the woods look creepy?" I point at the black trunks and dense wet foliage, tendrils of fog crawling toward us over gnarled roots. "A little lions-and-tigers-and-bears-y?" I joke, alluding, as I will again on this trip, to Dorothy's pilgrimage to Oz.

She shrugs. "Let's go the shorter way," she says.

"I don't know." I shake my head slowly, staring, mesmerized. How is it a twelve-year-old is not frightened, when I am seeing every sinister forest ever imagined? The clawing limbs that snatch at poor Snow White, making her panic and bolt further into darkness, the vampire-infested trees of *Salem's Lot,* the *Inferno*'s bleak wood of suicides: Walt Disney, Stephen King, Dante. Turn back, they all warn, and I have to agree.

"Sorry," I say. "I think we have to go the long way." We pick up our packs and say hearty things about how short a distance, really, is six kilometers, how the road goes down not up, how soon—no more than an hour—we'll arrive.

All day we've remarked that when the trail has diverged from the narrow mountain road, markers have been placed with wonderful sensitivity to the needs of those who are walking: not so often that they condescend, nor so infrequently that they inspire anxiety. Just exactly when we've wanted confirmation that we haven't strayed from the track, we've seen a tree trunk or rock painted with double red stripes. Now, in the gloom, suddenly we lose the trail. We walk in a wide circles over the hill we're descending, both of us bent over to see a slash of paint on one of the boulders that break through the grass, but find none. As unbearable as it is to backtrack when we're so tired and eager to arrive at our night's rest, we turn around to retrace our steps, only to discover ourselves defeated by our own circles.

"Shit," I say, losing my composure in spite of myself. "Okay," I say. "Okay. Okay. Let's just keep ourselves pointed downhill. We'll hit a road, we have to, and then the road will lead to the town."

Sarah nods, says nothing. After a few minutes of silent walking we find that we've unwittingly stumbled into a farmer's backyard: a pen filled with goats, a man in coveralls. "Hello," I say, and the man looks up.

"*Pas de pélerins,*" he answers.

"I don't need lodging," I say, grateful to be able to speak even my clumsy French. "I just want to know if you can point me back onto the road."

He says nothing.

"*Nous sommes perdues,*" I add, almost enjoying the drama of such an announcement. We are lost.

He smiles, nods. "*Visibilité très mauvaise,*" he says, and he directs us, speaking quickly and, to me, unintelligibly.

"*Je ne comprends pas,*" I interject each time he pauses, feeling humbled, humiliated, stupid. And then he begins again, pointing.

"It's just that I can't see where I'm going," I explain. "*Et je suis avec ma fille. Nous sommes fatiguées.*" I'm with my daughter and we're tired. He looks at me for a long moment, then drops his arm and calls to another man, whom I hadn't noticed leaning against a truck parked by the shed. They speak quickly, low, urgent words I don't understand, and the man shrugs and gets into the truck. He pulls out onto the track where we're standing, stops in front of us, and gets out. Then he comes around, opens the passenger door, and shoves aside a heap of clutter.

"*Merci,*" I say, and I look at Sarah, newly catechized

about the evils of the world, cautioned just two days ago in preparation for this trip: "Stick to your mother," her father said, "and don't talk to strange men"—warnings made over my protestations: "It's not like that there. I've been on the road before and it's safe. You know I wouldn't take her somewhere that wasn't safe." Sarah's face registers a brief look of fear, and in it I see a calculation, an assessment of me, her mother: too trusting, too naive.

"Come on." I contradict all the years of programming, force her to do the very thing every child is told never to do, get into a stranger's car. "It's all right."

The man slams the door, walks around the front. "I know this is weird, but it's okay," I tell Sarah again in the brief moment we're alone in the car. "I promise." She nods, curt, her face closed to my scrutiny. I try to imagine the thoughts behind her eyes, none of them reassuring. He gets in and begins to drive. The road leaps up out of the fog and into his headlights. It twists and loops and seems leagues longer than what I guessed from the maps, but each time I try to imagine him as a possible predator, I remind myself that we walked out of the fog and asked for help. He didn't stalk us but sighed and nodded at our need.

"Roncesvalles," he announces suddenly, and pulls up short. He gets out to open the passenger door and then, following Sarah, I slip out.

"*Merci. Merci. Merci beaucoup beaucoup.*" I wring his hand with overwrought gratitude, resist the urge to embrace him for being what I wanted him to be: a kind stranger, the antidote to living in New York City where we must preach suspicion to our children. He nods and looks away, embarrassed by the hot vehemence of my hand.

"Roncesvalles," he says again, and he points to a meager clutch of buildings.

Having walked today for eleven hours, having seen few travelers and little of the road itself, separately and together, silently and aloud, Sarah and I have fantasized about this town, picturing not a mere refuge, a bed and meal, but a whole mecca of shops and twinkling lights, choices of restaurants and inns, a photo booth as well a phone booth, voice of husband and of father, a fireplace and a glass of red wine, magazines and MTV and a surfeit of hot water and thick towels: an array of comforts to erase the hours of damp and chill. What we find instead is history: an ancient pilgrim hospital where many suffered and many died, a stone church sinking under centuries of petitions, a king's tomb and another king's silo, a battlefield, a monastery.

"Why are the signs in Spanish?" Sarah says, looking at a poster advertising a concert of choral music.

"Well," I say, "we are in Spain."

"Since when are we in Spain?"

"Since back there somewhere. I think around the time we were trying to decide which path to follow. That signpost by the woods."

"But," she says, a child familiar with the effusive state boundary markers: "Welcome to the Keystone State!" Her voice is sharp with disappointment. "But I wanted, for a moment, to stand with a foot in either country."

"Oh," I say. "I'm sorry, sweetie. I guess, well I guess I wasn't paying attention." My daughter looks at me, her expression of betrayal making her look suddenly younger. "Besides," I go on, "you did. At some point you did have a foot in either country."

"But I didn't know that I did." And therefore, her frown tells me, it didn't really happen. Does anything transpire outside of consciousness?

One disappointment follows another; the worst is dinner. At La Posada, the only hotel in Roncesvalles, with its chilly, stark rooms and surly-staffed restaurant, we have to wait until nine for a table, and then the food we are served is overcooked and highly salted. Sarah, a vegetarian, picks among the lumps on her plate, inspecting each darkly.

"Dessert?" I ask, and she makes a face.

"Let's just go to bed."

Thursday, July 25, 2002. 6:00 a.m. Roncesvalles.
I wake in a state of profound alienation and anxiety from a vivid dream in which I attend a conference that takes place in a citadel in the middle of a vast empty landscape. There I encounter a writer who looks exactly like me. We accost one another in a long hallway of closed doors, each of us bearing an armful of books, all of them written by me. At least I see my face on the dust jackets of the ones she carries. As we stare at each other, I lose the ability to determine which of us is the actual me. Having protested to this stranger that I am me, as proved by my carrying books I wrote, I realize that this proves nothing. The books in her arms are mine, too.

Up, scrubbing my face over the sink, I remind myself that one of the things I value about pilgrimage is the psychic violence of an experience that separates us from comfort and familiarity and context, all the habits we didn't know we held so dear. The act itself is not dramatic—putting one foot in front of the other—but it can wreak inner havoc. I try to quell fears by sorting and folding our clothes, by selecting a few more items to discard. Absurdly, I am carrying my unfinished novel with me, chapters I've written and those I've sketched out on index cards. I weigh the heavy envelope in my hand. The pages exist at home on disks, both on my computer's hard drive and on backup floppies, and yet I can't bring myself to leave the pages behind. What if, on this road, a perfect sentence were to arrive? In fact, isn't this why I walk the road, one sublime sentence my destination: words I've waited for all my life, the ones that in my dreams answer every question, redeem every hurt? I can't be caught unready, without the right page on which to insert the mystical gift. I replace the big envelope in the pack.

Sarah sleeps, and would sleep longer, but I rouse her. Already, only two days into the trip, a pattern has been established: I wake at six o'clock, fold and refold, pack and pace and stare, sort and repack, and then, when I can wait no longer, I sit beside her on her bed and call her name. Gently, I touch her hands, her feet. "Hi," I say. "Hello. We have to get going."

"Where are the pictures?" she asks, yawning, dressed for breakfast.

"Which pictures?"

"The pictures of me. The ones from the photo booth."

"You had them last night."

"Yeah, but now I don't." She looks under the bed and gets up from the floor, obviously distraught. How can she—we—have lost these priceless photographs? Images that were not merely good, not flattering but *right*, because in them she recognized herself, saw the self she wanted to see. We search the room thoroughly; I unfold and refold, fan the pages of every book and magazine.

"Maybe we left them in the dining room?" Maybe, last night when we were so tired, she never picked them up after she set them aside to eat.

We leave and lock the room, walk slowly through the dim hall and down the darker stair, scanning every corner. In the dining room we interrogate the waitress, the same who brought us our previous meal, and I even go back to the kitchen, the bar. Using fragments of three languages and a few pantomimes, I tell everyone who works at La Posada that we've lost some photographs, that we want very much to find them.

Back at the table, I spread jam on cold toast. "Maybe someone found them, and that person thought they were so pretty, he couldn't not keep them." I say this feeling a little ill, imagining too clearly a Spanish Humbert with my daughter's face caught in his billfold.

Sarah lifts her shoulders. She sips her cocoa and looks away. She won't allow herself to cry over the loss; crying is not what the invulnerably cool and lovely nymph in the picture would do.

We finish the last of the toast and go back to the room, where she sits on the bed. "I think we really have to leave now," I say. "I know you feel bad, and I do, too, but we can't keep looking."

"I know. I know."

Once more we walk slowly through the shadowy halls, and then we are outside, where the sun is brilliant, each wet leaf sparkles as if to tell us not to lose perspective: Beauty is in abundance.

Roncesvalles has no shops that sell provisions, so we set off with only peanuts and candy, a bottle of water. Will the next town have a market? How far along the road is the next town? The next pump with potable water? We talk to the man at the tiny tourist office, and to whomever we meet on the road, and the subjects are always the same, information revealing as the currency of greatest value. This is always true, of course, but it's interesting to have the questions change from what book to read, what stock to watch, what proposition to support, to where can we find water, food, lodging.

The road divides forest from pasture and, worn into the earth by centuries of walkers, dips down so low in places that it becomes a green trench, the surrounding country so high that we cannot see it.

"We're in sync," Sarah announces, after a long silence. I am about to ask how, when I look at her and see her eyes trained on our feet. "I didn't—I was careful not to try to change my walking to fit yours," she says. "We just gradually came together." She smiles and I beam back, what pleasure in this tiny convergence, pedestrian in every sense, yet it rings with significance. The path is graveled, with a satisfying crunch that amplifies each step; our two sets of footfalls lose their identification, separate and then realign, a kind of music.

"When I go for a run," I say, "I like this kind of track the best. I like to hear my feet strike, the rhythm of it."

"Me, too," Sarah says. She follows the red way markers, often seeing them before I do and taking pride in her quick eye.

At Burguete, we buy bread and sweets from a bakery, fruit, cheese, yogurt, and a prepaid phone card from a little market. Sarah sits on a bench while I struggle with the public phone. The twenty-euro card doesn't work—either that, or I can't make it work—but after a few tries, my credit card is accepted. I hear my husband's sleepy voice, say hello to the younger children, Walker and Julia, then hand Sarah the phone, curious to hear whether she'll tell her father about the truck ride, but she doesn't.

"Yes," she says. "Yes. I am."

Am *what*, I wonder but don't ask. Having fun?
Using the camera? Taking care?

"Today we can either end at Zubiri or at Larrasoaña," I
say as we leave Viscarret. It's just after noon; according
to the guide, we've covered twelve kilometers. Zubiri is
another nine; Larrasoaña is fourteen more.

"Larrasoaña," my daughter says, and she says it
again when we're regarding Zubiri across a highway,
from a distance of two kilometers. Having walked
these two days, we're converts to the footpath, whenever
possible avoiding contact with—and consciousness of—
roads with their speeding cars and trucks, a parallel and
alien universe.

"Are you sure?" I ask.

"I'm sure."

The day's remaining kilometers are ugly and unin-
spiring. Cleaving to a concrete culvert, then an asphalt
road, then disappearing into woods, the road to
Larrasoaña wends along the southern bank of the River
Arga, whose water we hear churning and rushing on our
right, but mostly can't see. We've walked ten hours
already today, tired enough that we don't bother to
admire Zubiri's Bridge of Rabies, around whose central

pier locals drive their livestock, as they have for centuries. Three revolutions cure or ward off the dread disease, a protection granted by the relics of St. Quiteria, interred in one of the structure's abutments.

"I think we may have made the wrong decision," I say to Sarah, who smiles.

"Yes," she says, cheerful, punch drunk. "We did." In the distance, across the still visible highway is a bar or a restaurant, and as we walk we try to read the name written on the sign, we imagine the good food it might, but probably doesn't, serve. But it's too far for us to make out the letters.

"It can't be too much farther," one of us reassures the other every kilometer or so, and we refer back to the guide, picking our way through the text as we trudge up a dry hillside pocked with little stones. Where is the river? Where is the river? Somewhere there is the sound of water—or is that the rustle of wind through dry leaves? That we cannot see what we hear underscores the disorientation of this second long day's end. Earlier we sacrificed two ponchos, two novels, a map, and a bottle of hand cream, and we've drunk all our water, so why do the packs remain so stunningly heavy?

We emerge from foliage to see not only the river but the Bandits' Bridge (named for those who ambush pilgrims at any such spots that give advantage to thieves), which leads directly into the main street of the town of Larrasoaña, dominated by its church. Just outside the sanctuary door, a young woman sits reading a guide written in English. I drop onto the bench next to her, too tired for any formality, and let the pack slide off. Sarah, by nature reserved—a child who in fact never needed to be cautioned about strangers—stands some five feet away.

"Is there a place to stay?" I ask without preamble.

"There's the refugio," the young woman answers.

"Restaurant?"

"A bar."

I nod. "Which way to the refuge?" There's only one street, but it goes in two directions, and we haven't the energy to take the wrong one. She points left. "Thanks," I say, standing and heaving up the pack. Then I turn around. "It isn't full, is it?" She shrugs.

The pilgrim refuge of Larrasoaña is run by the mayor of the tiny town, a man whose name is Santiago, and whose saint's day is, even more improbably, this very night, to be celebrated (we learn from other English-speaking pilgrims, loitering in the entry) with wine and cookies. Perhaps the day accounts for his enthusiasm as he records our names in his ledger, stamps and signs our credenciales with a flourish. As must be obvious by my apologetic head shaking and repeated *no comprendo*, I can't converse in Spanish, but Santiago is one of those people who goes at a problem like a cheerful battering ram, hammering away at what he thinks is perhaps stubbornness rather than ignorance, talking and talking, never acknowledging that I cannot be made to understand him.

In his office at the refuge are photographs of Santiago in his earlier, itinerant life. Apparently he has walked the whole road at least three times, as proved by his laminated *credenciales* displayed under photographs of an ascetic wearing a monk's robe and carrying a staff. An Old Testament beard makes it hard to connect these images to the clean-shaven, portly, and avuncular man waving from across the room, but it is he. "Camera! Camera!" he insists, and I pull out our pocket flash, thinking he's offering to take a picture of my daughter and me, but, no, it's his own image he wants us to record and to send him, once the film is developed. He presses his business card into my hand, folding my fingers around it, and he gives another to Sarah. Perhaps now that he is old and no longer walking the road himself, such mementos have acquired a vicarious power, for the little room is filled with pictures of him and his guests at the refuge. Using my clumsy syllables and signs, I promise to send him what he wants: a copy of each of the two photographs, one taken by Sarah, of

Santiago and me standing under his red flag with the gold crown, and one taken by me, of Santiago and Sarah.

As I'm putting away the camera, a man knocks and comes in to ask a question. "Do you speak English?" I ask him as he finishes speaking with Santiago and turns to leave.

"A little."

"Is there food here in town, a restaurant?"

"A pilgrim menu down the street," he says, pointing. "There's only the one bar. You can't miss it."

I thank him. "What time do they begin serving?" I think to ask as he's leaving.

"Eight."

By chance—by the kind of luck that has protected my every visit to Spain—the two spaces left at the refuge are in a separate room, a private room for just the two of us, so we are spared what Sarah has dreaded, a dormitory filled not with kids, like at camp, but grownup strangers. There's no private bathroom, no television, no towels, no chairs. Just the floor, and the pallets, and piles of clear plastic garment storage bags filled, unaccountably, with what look like costumes, Halloween or Mardi Gras finery. I stand for some minutes, fascinated by this unexpected trove of disguises tucked in a bare room, on a cobbled street, in the midst of a journey undertaken with an opposite agenda—that of stripping away layers. I stand staring, struck by a fancy: People have passed through this place leaving their false selves behind, taken them off, folded and left them here, a growing pile for the next wayfarer to contemplate.

"Weird," says Sarah, from one of the pallets.

"Very."

Above the costumes are a stack of folded blankets and linens, and I make up the little beds, and we lie down to wait for dinner. "I think," I say on my back, feet in the air, "I think I'm not going to take my shoes off, because then I'll have to put them back on, and I might not be able to stand it."

"Uh-huh," Sarah says absently from behind the tattered cover of a *Teen Vogue*. Despite their collective weight, and my refusal to share this burden, she's carrying several junior versions of the standard fashion magazines: *Elle Girl*, *Seventeen*, *YM*, and others. Camp is over; school looms; Sarah is entering the seventh grade, entering into an agony of self-consciousness. She studies glossy ads with the intensity of someone preparing for a critical examination, which isn't far from the truth.

I get up to look at the garment bags. I'd like to open them, touch the sequins and the bits of velvet trim, the feathers, but the bags are secured against such trespass, each zipper closed with a tiny silver padlock.

Hungry, we enter the tavern at eight o'clock exactly, and find its three long tables already filled, benches crowded with the people staying at our refuge, including the young woman who directed us from outside the church. She moves aside to give Sarah room at the end of her bench, and I take the place opposite. A sign over the little bar offers a pilgrim dinner for ten euros; the meal includes two courses, a drink, and a dessert. If it wasn't clear last evening in Roncesvalles, it is tonight: Spain is not a land for vegetarians. We navigate the limited menu with help from the young woman, whose name I never ask because she doesn't offer it, not even after learning ours. Like the man who gave us a lift in his truck, she proves invaluable, convincing the tavern to produce an omelet and fried potatoes for Sarah.

"Do you live in the States?" I ask her. No, she's from Wisconsin, but she lives in Valladolid, teaching English as a second language.

"To adults, or younger students?"

"Everyone," she says. "Old people, toddlers. I love it," she adds, and I nod. She has a face pinched by unhappiness, but her features relax into something like prettiness as she translates among the tablemates, allowing us to share our experiences with each other: the towns where we began our journeys, how much of the road we hope to cover, and our ages. *"Doce,"* she tells everyone. Sarah is twelve. Everyone nods appreciatively; one woman holds her glass of wine aloft, and Sarah hunches her shoulders in embarrassment. But I'm glad for the toast, happy to see strangers confirm that my daughter is among the very few who might, at twelve, persevere on such a road. As I raise my glass I'm aware, as I wasn't at home, of my leap of faith in trusting that I knew my daughter well enough to bet that she could and would walk with me along this road, uncomplaining, open to the experience, to the alienation, the reorientation. I hope these are useful to her now, on the cusp of adolescence, the profound realignments required on the journey from child to adult.

Upstairs at the refugio, having avoided Santiago's wine and cookies and boisterous songs of celebration, we find that in our absence our room has grown cold. I sort once again through the stack of blankets until I find a heavy wool one for each of us. I come upon a clean sheet sewn into a bag, and I give it to Sarah. "Here," I say, "this will keep the blanket from scratching." Sarah slips inside the white rectangle, like a letter into an envelope, I think, reminded abruptly of a few lines written by St. Thérèse of Lisieux to her sister Pauline. Apologizing for being secretive about her failing health (she was, at twenty-three, dying of tuberculosis), Thérèse assured her older sister that whatever she may have withheld about the "envelope," her body, the "letter" within, her soul, belonged to Pauline.

"Do people walk the road backward?" Sarah asks, her eyes closed.

"I don't know," I say, misinterpreting the question to imagine a pilgrim headed west while walking literally backward, facing the road he has covered rather than the steps he anticipates. "Maybe someone has, as a form of penance."

"Why would that be penance?" Sarah asks, after a silence.

"Well, I don't know—not seeing where you're going would make it harder."

She laughs. "Mom," she says, "I meant starting in Santiago and heading back this way, in the opposite direction as ours."

"Oh, I don't know. I don't think so." Curiously, it's harder for me to imagine walking east, toward sunrise and birth, rather than west with my face averted from sunset and from death, the bright fire of the sun god's chariot descending into the waves with a hiss.

Overwrought by this long day, I am more than usually attuned to the topic that consumes me: mortality, the impossible and inescapable truth of human life. How can it be that we are souls trapped in flesh, spirits bound to matter? These bodies we have, the same that grant us every pleasure and every perception, fail us; they break down; they age and die. Isn't that why we walk this road—to rehearse the awful truth we know and yet cannot believe? And I've upped the ante this time, I think, watching my firstborn as she sleeps. We weep at the birth of our children, mothers and fathers, too, in part because it's death we bring into the world—creatures whom we love as we love ourselves, even more, regarding them as purer, innocent, and vulnerable. And yet flesh of our flesh heading inexorably to the same destination.

How often do we, as parents, leap to the last and most dire bargain, even when it's not required? My life for hers; take me, not my child; take my kidney, my lung, a lobe of my liver—what price could be too high? I watch Sarah turn in her sleep, wind the shroudlike sheet around her legs, but only for as long as I can stand to. Then I unfold and drop the heavy blanket over her body, and change her from prophesy back into a little girl.

Two

Friday, July 26, 2002. 5:30 a.m. Larrasoaña.

July days are long, sun in the sky until nine o'clock and then up again before six. Outside the window of our small bedroom beams scatter from between the trees onto a pretty scene: horses and sheep in small paddocks, hills and streams, an uncomplicated vista. Already, at six, the refuge is nearly empty, pilgrims having set out early to avoid afternoon heat. I take a cold shower and sneak a quick rub from a towel hanging by the sink. A persnickety trespasser, I smell the towel first.

At the tavern where we ate the previous night, we have what has become our standard breakfast: coffee for me, cocoa for Sarah, bread, butter, and jam. Then we set out with a few provisions, heading for Pamplona on what should be a short day compared to the two that preceded it. But perhaps we are too focused on this relative brevity, because the city that should be closer seems ever farther.

"I keep thinking of Dorothy," I say to Sarah, "when she falls into the poppies, the Emerald City visible but out of reach."

She nods. "I've thought of that scene a bunch of times since we started."

"The third day is the worst," proclaims an older gentleman we pass. "My son did this, and he told me the third day is the worst." The phrase sticks in our heads, and we repeat it, not just on this, the third day, but on the fourth and fifth days, which will prove, in fact, far harder.

At midday, tired and footsore and dizzy with sun, in a hamlet identified by our guide as Zuriain, I unpack my bag and leave my alternate pair of shoes on a bench, not without a pang. Certainly I'm carrying less useful and more burdensome things—my novel-in-progress, for example, but I can't discard the pages, which are for me as valuable as my passport: proof of who I am, wandering on a strange track. For the same reason, Sarah suffers under her magazines, templates of who she might be, guides to the future more necessary than our travel literature, whose uselessness is proven just outside Pamplona, where we read a map upside down and falter in the suburb of Burlada. The road is so easy to follow, the trail markers so clear and frequent, that maps are not only unnecessary but even, at times, confusing. It's a problem of transition between the literal, a dusty, winding path we walk, and the conceptual, a clean, aerial, and oddly misleading representation. Lost, I assuage my anxiety and frustration by accessing a wad of euros from an automated bank teller. We flirt, briefly, with the idea of getting on a bus—how wonderful to sit and be carried somewhere, anywhere. But we walk on, accosting one after another stranger, to whom we show our crumpled map, and are finally pointed in the right direction. After another three hot, cranky kilometers we reach the walls of Pamplona, not the same that fell to Charlemagne, but ancient enough. Trees sprout from between their immense blocks; vines creep and snarl.

"Pretty," I say, meaning how the green looks against blackened stone, how vibrant and alive.

"What's pretty?" Sarah walks with her head bent, her eyes on the ground. She's tired.

"The wall," I say. She looks up and squints, says nothing.

The guide we are using divides the pilgrim road into thirty stages, averaging twenty-five kilometers each, and cuts through Pamplona to break at a little town called Cizur, some five kilometers to the west. But the attraction of a city, even a city as small as Pamplona, is too great to allow us to walk on without stopping, so we quit in the early afternoon, checking into the hotel, La Perla, whose most famous guest and his enthusiasm for the bull run has created a whole tourist industry.

"No wonder he shot himself," I say to Sarah, falling onto the bed.

"Who?" she asks. "What do you mean?"

"Hemingway."

"He shot himself?"

"I was just making a joke about the hotel."

Sarah looks around. "He shot himself here?"

"No, no, years later, in Idaho, I think. It had nothing to do with the hotel. I was just acknowledging that the room is ..." I stop.

"Depressing?" she suggests.

"In a word."

The shower—the amenity for which I've justified paying sixty-eight euros for our double room—is almost hot, but the sprayer head won't stay put. Attached to a plastic handle and hose, it drops from the overhead bracket and whacks me in the face three times before I devise a method of pinning it to the tile wall with my knee as I try to lather up my sweat-soaked hair.

Without a television, the room offers only one possibility for entertainment; a window opens onto an air shaft filled with laundry lines, flapping clothes, underwear, and other open windows, all targets at which Sarah fires projectiles of crumpled paper and candy wrappers. Few hit their mark, and I don't consider stopping her pursuit of silly fun, in short supply on this "not-exactly-a-vacation," as she calls it.

Having bathed and changed, we wander through town, window-shopping during the siesta lull. Peering into a boutique, Sarah sees a belt she likes, one that is cool and chic and, hopefully, not available at home, and we note the shop's location and plan to return. Sarah is palpably reassured by the town, by the solid stones of civilization, the bright windows of commerce.

Another hour remains before stores reopen, so we go to the cathedral and its adjoining museum, neither of which are particularly interesting, even to me, who is usually ravenous for every church and font, eager to splash holy water on my head. Would it be different without the watchful presence of my daughter, her ready skepticism? For the first time in my life, I'm struck by the remoteness of the icons. Sitting in Mary's lap, Jesus stares solemnly into his future, into a death foretold, looking stiff and sad and false, rendered not as a child but as an awkward little man. After three days of walking, two sets of footsteps falling in and out of rhythm, three days of continuing even when tired because there is no choice, the cathedral seems superfluous to what has become an essential exercise in faith. And the questions posed by the walk—How much can I carry and for how long? Where do my thoughts go when I am silent? What aspects of my life back home do I miss, and what are the ones I am glad to escape?—seem more immediately religious, more uniting of spirit and matter than the time we spend fidgeting in dank pews.

We return to the boutique and buy the belt, then wander as we wait for dinner. When, at nine o'clock, the restaurants at last open, we choose a Chinese place, figuring fried rice might be the only vegetarian option in Pamplona, and enjoying the cultural collision of the gaudy dragon ceiling panels, the pink napkins folded into swans, and, outside the window, a view of the bullring.

Saturday, July 27, 2002. 6:00 a.m. Pamplona.
At nineteen, I discovered the narcotic of movement. Traveling with a pack from city to city, Paris to Madrid to Barcelona and back to Paris then Vienna, on and on—two months of unlimited travel on a Eurail youth pass—I was happiest on the trains, staring out the

window, anticipating a destination rather than experiencing it. Becoming versus being: Was it on the trains that I began to understand the major conflict of my life? Inspired by my relationship with my mother, my determination to transform myself into the object of her desire, I never saw myself as a being, human or otherwise, but as a work-in-progress, larval, as inferior to what I might become as a groping caterpillar to a gravity-defying butterfly. Even knowing this about myself, I am still always disappointed by arrival, eager to depart, to get to the place I haven't yet reached, the one that seems as if it might really offer transcendence.

Bored by sights, bored by shopping. No, worse, made anxious by these pastimes, for shouldn't I be leaving again, heading toward my destiny? That's my problem, I think, sorting and packing and trying to let Sarah sleep, I confuse the two: destination and destiny.

I rouse Sarah with a promise of seeing a touristy reenactment of the bull run. At eight o'clock, a dozen animals will be chased through the streets by actors dressed as matadors, and at that hour we are standing on the periphery of the Plaza del Castillo, waiting, listening for the approach of hooves. But either I misread the map, or I've misunderstood the woman at the tourist information office, for the streets remain empty, no bulls appear.

"I'm sorry," I say. "It's probably not the best time to mention this, as far as we are from home, but I'm crummy with maps."

"No you're not," she says, loyal.

West of Pamplona we cross through fields of wheat, hot and dusty and gorgeous, and then begin to ascend the foothills of the Sierra del Perdón. After the town of Zariquiegui, under whose pump we douse our hot heads, we see the Molino de Viento, a wind farm on the ridged crest. The line of mills turn, white and sleek and utterly modern, and yet it is hard to walk toward them without thinking of Don Quixote, without asking myself what it is I'm tilting at. According to our map, the altitude of the pass over the sierra is 734 meters, a steady rocky climb from Pamplona, now twelve kilometers behind us. It seems impossible that in a mere four days we can have walked from cool mist into such intense heat. The white-hot eye of the sun glares down, imparting scrutiny as well as swelter, and I have the sense of measuring up to neither.

After a series of false arrivals, one peak hidden behind another, we reach the summit of Perdón and are immediately greeted by a reassuring sight: an

Englishman with a camper, a card table set with a basket of cookies and another of hard candies.

"Welcome," he says, opening his arms in a messianic gesture. "I am one of the surprises of the *camino*." He offers us a choice of cold or hot beverages: lemonade, cola, coffee, tea. "Are you Americans?" he asks, and I say that we are.

"You must be here because of Shirley MacLaine," he says, looking me up and down.

"No," I say, bristling immediately. "What can you mean?" He explains that Shirley MacLaine has written a book about her journey on the camino, one that included her reliving past lives, and I shake my head, change the topic to one that is less likely to make me rude to this kind, if unwittingly insulting, person. "Do you live in Spain?" I ask.

"I do now." As he explains, this gentleman (like the young woman in Larrasoaña, he doesn't give his name and I don't ask it) has dedicated himself to helping pilgrims. In the mornings he parks and offers sustenance from his traveling kitchen. Afternoons, he drives along the road, looking for people who cannot make it to the next town.

"How many do you pick up in a day?" I ask him.

"Half a dozen." He tells me he travels no farther west than León, because those who make it that far—some 375 kilometers west of Pamplona—can go the distance to Santiago: Their feet have toughened up.

A very tempting subject for a magazine profile, I conclude, this wry and courtly, quirky Brit; he has charm as well as zeal, and I am tempted to ask what it was he did before he undertook this calling, what drives his mission to help faltering pilgrims. I imagine the accompanying photograph: he standing before his rust-pocked camper, the panorama spread behind him, the great windmills turning above. But what would be the cost of transforming him into content, another morsel to be consumed by the endlessly voracious readers of profiles, the culture's indiscriminate appetite? I decide that I don't want to ask the questions, write the piece, even reveal my trade.

"Can we see Puente la Reina from here?" I ask.

"No." He shakes his head. "It's hidden just beyond that hill." He points west, into the hazy hot shimmering plain. A road twists past one, two, three towns, then disappears. "Uterga, Muruzábal, Obanos," he names the towns we can see. "Then, behind that last hill, Puente la Reina. You'll get there by five. Even if you stop to rest, you'll get there."

I nod. "Can I offer you a little donation. For future cookies?"

He nods. "Thank you," he says, but he shakes his

head when he unfolds the twenty-euro bill. He hands it back. "Too much," he says.

"Please let me. It's, um, it's something I believe in, too, the camino."

He squints at me, considering, then nods. "Petrol," he says. "I'll buy petrol with this."

Sarah and I set off down the hill. Rocks loosened under our feet tumble ahead of our descent. What did I mean, I ask myself. Or, better, why? Why do I believe in the road? This fourth day forces the question, because it is hot, and the trail is rugged, because my knees and ankles ache, and above all these discomforts, because I've brought a companion—a hostage—to my belief.

As we have on previous days, we enter a town—is it Uterga? Perhaps it's Muruzábal, during the dead hot quiet of siesta, when even the dogs seem under a spell, lying motionless in whatever shade they can find. Some of these Navarese towns are quaint, seemingly untouched by centuries; others are graceless: broken stone walls and junked dusty automobiles. But in the middle of afternoon siesta, with shops and bars closed, curtains drawn, they all partake of the same silence— spooky to big city dwellers, as if we'd fallen into one of those deserted plazas in a de Chirico painting, every sun-washed corner sparkling and sinister. What can this abandoned quiet mean? Surely something more ominous than naps is unfolding. We sit, exhausted and dirty, on the stones around the pump, listening to the loud splash of the water we summon. Several times we douse our hot heads.

Stupidly, I allowed us to leave Pamplona with water and candy but no food. Expecting that I could buy provisions in Guenduláin or Zariquiegui—towns that look like towns on the maps, towns in fact referred to as towns in the guide—I panic inwardly when they turn out to be no more than a clutch of buildings, a bar but no market. At Obanos, also without a market, we go into the bar and discover tables crowded with sunburned footsore pilgrims who have clearly given up for the day, drinking beer as they peel off filthy socks to inspect their blisters. We buy water and popsicles, a tiny can of roasted, hulled sunflower seeds. "Do you want to stop?" I ask my daughter, but she shakes her head.

"Let's keep going," she says, her lips red from the popsicle. "Let's get to the city." Pamplona has convinced her that civilization exists; if we walk another hour, another two hours, we will find it.

"Okay," I say, and we struggle forward, but the afternoon heat teaches us—too late—the wisdom of walking early in the day. At three o'clock, the sun is so intense that a hat and sunglasses cannot protect our eyes, and we find ourselves scuttling like insects from one sliver of shade to the next. There are no trees, but the local farmers stack their hay bales one on top of another, making hay fortresses two or even three stories tall, all bearing witness to previous walkers. Pressed to the side of one of these, we discover that someone has tunneled into it to make a latrine.

"Poor farmer," Sarah says.

Flies buzz, stalks of hay prick through our shirts and itch, but, too tired to care, we sit against the bales, legs folded into the margin of shade, and give ourselves ten minutes, checking our watches as they evaporate.

"The first hotel," Sarah says when Puente la Reina appears in the distance, gold as Dorado.

"I promise."

"Unless it's a dump," she qualifies.

"Right."

But it isn't. We get a room with a television and a phone that works. Sarah stares at a synchronized swimming competition telecast from Berlin; I dump dirty socks and underpants into the sink, soak them in hot water before even trying to wash them. Sitting on the twin bed next to hers, I unwrap a tiny bar of soap and watch the TV. Two slick and lovely bodies fall in unison into an expanse of impossible blue.

"Do you want the first shower?" I offer, but Sarah says nothing. "Okay, I'll go." I force my voice toward cheer.

Under the stream of water I sit on the floor of the bathtub, letting it fall like hot rain on my bent neck. I've learned something on this trip; days of walking with my daughter, the two of us alone together, have taught me something. I'm a little afraid of my child: her beauty and her silences, her ability to wound me. "What are you thinking?" I've asked too often on this walk. Luckily—lucky for her and for me—she has too much integrity to allow such clumsy intrusions. "Nothing," she says, and even, once, "My thoughts are mine."

Eyes closed, I ask myself if, in fact, part of the decision to bring Sarah with me was to acknowledge my fear of her, to walk with it. To admit that perhaps I will never learn how not to impose my history with my mother onto my love for my children. With her shining dark hair and blue eyes, her long legs and unconscious slender grace, Sarah is the girl my mother wanted, exactly so. This frightens me sometimes, as if my longing to be desired has finally found this profound expression: I could not make myself into the daughter of my mother's fantasies, not in her lifetime. But then, after she died, mysteriously and unexpectedly, I did make a girl in that image.

What are you thinking? I will try to exile the question. I will try to not voice it, even if I can't help thinking it. *Are you leaving me?* Those would be the honest words, the ones I really mean: Are you forsaking me with your silence?

Or are you just too tired to speak, my fierce child, who carried a heavy pack for ten hot hours?

Having promised that we wouldn't go out, that we'd eat in the hotel, I'm told downstairs that the restaurant is full. Without a reservation, we cannot eat in it.

"But we're staying here," I try, "at the hotel." I present our room key as proof.

The maître d' shakes his head. "It's only a little way into the center of town." He points. "A kilometer or two, no more."

Ad-vil, Ad-vil, the syllables repeat themselves in my head as we walk those two kilometers only to discover the reason for the hotel restaurant's refusing us: It's fiesta time; every restaurant is full. The town heaves with music and beer, carnival rides, street vendors hustling and hawking. But not a table to be found. Who will have us? Only bars with dry meat sandwiches. In one such place, a drunken man tries to pull me into a dance, and I leave hastily, dragging Sarah by the wrist.

"We're going back to the hotel and eating there," Sarah says after another block of failures.

"We don't have a reservation."

"I don't care." Her eyes are bright, filled with hot recriminations.

"All right," I agree, close to crying myself. Having walked an extra hour, we trudge back. But the maître d' is adamant; the restaurant cannot accommodate two more diners.

Sarah cries. Tears she was too proud to show me she spills for the maître d' with electrifying effect. Within seconds we are seated, given menus and a basket of bread, pats of butter perspiring on a saucer. All around us, locals drink and toast one another, young men dressed in traditional fiesta wear, white shirts and red kerchiefs. They are so loud as to make conversation impossible, but it doesn't matter, as we are too tired to talk.

Sunday, July 28, 2002. Puente la Reina.
I wake soon after five o'clock, going to the open window to feel the scrubbed socks and underpants hanging from the sill, everything bone dry in the arid wind that has cracked my lips and parched my hair. I fold and sort and

pack our bags. Clearly the only way to survive the heat is to avoid walking in the afternoons, to start by six and finish by two. But I can't wake Sarah, not after yesterday, not when she is so tired. Here is a critical factor I failed to consider, the biological clock of an adolescent, which leaves her alert at night, unconscious at dawn.

By eight we are having a good breakfast, and I pocket extra rolls, an apple and a pear and a few single serving packets of jam. I pay too much for bottled water from the hotel concession, but it's Sunday, and I'm worrying that markets will be closed. Today we will walk to Estella, only nineteen kilometers, but they will be hot, and very dry. And there will be hills, more hills. It's our fifth day, the one on which we'll quit, but I don't know that yet.

The streets of Puente la Reina are strewn with plastic cups. The yeasty smell of spilled beer rises from the gutters. Carnival rides, tawdry in daylight, are folded for transport, and a compact street sweeper—those like we have at home in New York would not fit through these old cobbled lanes—pushes litter before it. Perhaps fiesta rearranges the week's usual schedule, because, in fact, the shops are open, and I buy bread and cheese and yogurt.

The bridge for which the city is named takes us back over the Arga, a river whose winding course we have crossed already twice before. We walk together in silence.

Sarah breaks it, saying, "There are people who go the whole way to what's it called?"

"Santiago?"

"Yeah, there."

"Yes."

She sighs gustily. "They must have a death wish."

"Do you think?"

She doesn't answer. Fascinated as I am by endurance, it suddenly occurs to me that perhaps I make the mistake of assuming others are as well. Am I guilty of projecting my psychic agenda onto everyone around me, even onto my child, to whom I owe protection? I steal glances at her, trying to gauge the level of her unhappiness, but her face is composed, unreadable.

At Cirauqui, eight kilometers into our day, we walk a stretch of Roman road bordered by cypress; it's the kind of experience I find at once reassuring and terrifying. Here are stones set in place two thousand years before, a road that, inanimate, endures. And here am I, sentient, overfilled with hopes and longings, and evanescent. My life added to my daughter's is a minute fraction of the life of a stone, and I've spent so much of that morsel already.

"One fifteen," Sarah says. This is perhaps her fifth announcement of the time.

I nod. Something is happening today: She is bored, or she is tired; maybe she is afraid. Can it be of me, I wonder. I am the parent she finds less solid and steady and predictable, and the one she is following from nowhere to nowhere. And she is the child who, when she was four or five and we walked together in New York, sometimes dropped my hand and refused to continue with me. "You don't know where we are!" she'd accuse. "You have no idea where we're going!" "I do," I'd say, explaining the course we'd taken. But she wouldn't trust me. She stamped her feet and even, once, sobbed before taking my hand and walking on, having at five no other choice.

I think of the kite I gave her when she was seven. She flew it on a short string, and it hung over our heads, fabric rippling in a perfect wind.

"Let it out," I said.

"No. It will get lost."

"It's no fun to fly a kite right over your head," I argued. "Let out some string."

She shook her head, and I bullied her into doing what she didn't want to do. I took the string wound on the stick, let it out, and let the kite soar. "Look!" I said. "See how pretty! How high!"

The string snapped, and she flew into a rage, actually holding her fists over her head. "Mom will get you a new one," I promised, retreating like a coward into the third person. "A better one."

"I loved that one. That one! The one you lost and broke!"

"I'm sorry. I am sorry. I'll get another."

"I am never never never going to let you touch my kite again," she screamed.

And she never has. Incautious, uncircumspect, too trusting, too impulsive, too open: The very qualities in me that she fears she also admires.

"Are you a conventional person?" she asks me now as we walk.

I shrug. "What do you think?"

"I think you're not."

"I think I'm not, too."

She nods, looking at me in the way I love: unabashed in her assessment. She's analyzing me and doesn't pretend otherwise. "I'm not going to be conventional, either," she says after a moment.

"Okay," I say.

The towns after Puente la Reina are filled with swooping, wheeling clouds of swallows. The buildings' eaves bear as many daubed nests as they can hold, and the small birds swarm around the roofs like insects. When a church bell gongs the hour, the noise sends them high into the air. Then they fall, with the silence.

"Pretty," I say.

"Creepy," Sarah replies.

As we walk I find myself rehearsing obsessively for the following day. Inevitably, we won't get an early start, and the hot afternoon portion will be twelve kilometers long, taking us through dry, treeless terrain, without a town, without a pump. How much water will I need to carry for two people? A gallon to be safe. A gallon which will add another eight pounds to my pack. As if to underscore the calculation, my left knee twangs with a new pain.

"Do you want to take a break?" I ask. "Under that bridge, in the shade?" Sarah looks where I point ahead to a small concrete span lifting the road over a dry creek bed.

She shrugs. "Do you?"

How uneven it is between us. Gamely, she's agreed to this trip, a mother-daughter adventure, and yet it's nothing she could have anticipated. What are the rules, I can feel her wonder as she looks at me. Is she allowed to agree that she's tired? That she wants to stop? What is the cost in admitting defeat, even so small a defeat? When I ask if I can carry her pack for a while, she says no.

"Because you're not tired, or because you're too proud?" Sarah squints, considering what it's not clear: the question, her mother, the slant of the sun, the time it will take to cover the last seven kilometers to Estella.

"Proud," she answers.

"Okay," I say, nodding. "I get that. I think of pride as my specialty among the seven deadly sins."

"How do you mean?"

"Well, I'm not particularly avaricious, I'm definitely not slothful, and I'm not overly lustful. Or, let's see, what's the one where you eat a lot—gluttonous. And I'm not an angry person. I mean, certain things make me angry, but anger doesn't stand between me and life." I pause. "How many is that?"

"Six, counting pride."

"Yeah, I always forget one. Oh, vanity. I'm not so vain."

"But you are proud."

"Yes."

Sarah tilts her head to one side. "Why is that bad?"

"Well, pride is tricky. It's useful, connected with will and achievement and pulling yourself up by your bootstraps and all that. But it's also dangerous."

"How?"

"Because—well, because you won't accept help when you need it. So it can separate you from other people, and the only hope humans have of happiness is each other. Pride is solitary. Lonely."

Sarah nods, says nothing, and we walk toward the shadow under the bridge. There are two large stones under the span, set like chairs against the smooth curve of the arch. It smells of urine here, a rank smell of the sort we no longer comment on. Any shade is valuable, enviable, no matter how distasteful under other circumstances. I lean against the cool, dank concrete.

Some of what I love about the road is its rewriting of life's priorities. Now that I exist in a world in which shade is the most valuable commodity, I am given a vision of myself, my old concerns set in relief against the new order. And of course this makes the road a journey home, a return to comfort and familiarity, each day another day closer.

As I sit on my stone, moving my toes carefully in my shoes, trying, without looking, to gauge the progress of my blisters, I see a coiling shape drop from above and hit the ground with a slap and a slither. Sarah screams and I jump, then laugh shakily, feeling adrenaline wash through my body, from my heart to my fingertips, tingling. "Harmless, harmless," I say. "The head isn't triangular." I watch the snake wind away toward a clump of weeds.

"Was it a garter snake?" Sarah says as its tail disappears.

"Something like that. It must have been winding along the bridge and then fallen off." We sit back down, musing about the resilience of the animal, whatever allowed it to endure a fall of twenty feet and keep going as if nothing had happened. What beautiful and sinister locomotion, and what loathing it inspires in us by not having limbs—legs. By its moving without walking.

Out from under the bridge, the sun hits with brutal force. Despite sunblock, we are burned, our skin gritty with dried sweat and dust, and we're exhausted. It's four in the afternoon, the dregs of this day's life, and we're eager for it to be over.

"Are you okay?" I ask, looking at Sarah's red cheeks.

"Uh-huh."

"Really okay?"

"I feel a little sick, but I'm all right."

Heat comes up from the ground and strikes our shins with the kind of radiant blast that emanates from an opened oven door. And it's Sunday, so when we come upon a metal sign on the outskirts of Lorca saying BAR, I warn Sarah that it might not be open. Under the word BAR an arrow points up a long flight of steps, each one shimmering malignly in the incredible heat. "It must be at least ninety degrees," I guess.

"It's a hundred."

"It's a hundred million." I drop my pack on the ground. "Sit here," I say to Sarah, "and I'll go up and see what's there."

A bar, as promised, with an air-conditioning unit humming in the window. I poke my head in the door to look for the now familiar, and beloved, poster illustrating the various kinds of popsicles and ice-cream bars kept in the freezer under the bar.

"Come on," I call down the steps. "There's popsicles!"

We drag our packs up the stairs and sit at a table in the smoke-filled bar. I get out the guide to look at what I've looked at perhaps ten times already today: the map for tomorrow's 20.4 hilly kilometers from Estella to Los Arcos. Villamayor is the midpoint; between it and Los Arcos is the dreaded twelve-kilometer stretch, no town, no shade, nothing but the one symbol for a pump, a promise not to be trusted when it's this dry and hot. I consider, as I have at various points, the idea of quitting early—two phases, fifty kilometers, short of our goal of Logroño. It's a hard thing to do, defying everything we're taught, every bromide we pass on to our children. In short, a bad precedent, a negative example—or is it? I think of all the dull books I've pursued to the last page, all the bad movies I refused to walk out on, even, once or twice, moribund friendships I refused to let die. Is this enlightened?

Sarah leans her hot face on one hand and licks her popsicle, grateful for this tiny reprieve. Though I know she's questioned what we're doing, found it dull at points, painful at others, she has never complained. I look at her.

"I know, I know," she says, misinterpreting my focus on her as an exhortation to hurry. "I'm almost done." She sits up straight, preparing herself for the idea of walking under the pack.

"What would you think," I ask, "of quitting two days early? Heading up to Bilbao tomorrow instead of on Wednesday?"

For a second, even less, she smiles, a huge smile that collapses immediately into a frown.

"It's because of me, isn't it?" she asks.

"No. I just don't think we're having much fun today. It's hard like it wasn't before, and tomorrow's going to be even harder. I planned this to be a good trip for us. I don't want it to turn into something we wish we weren't doing."

"But," she says, suspicious, "don't we have to keep walking? Don't we have to get to where we said we would?" I look at her, wondering if this is the mantra she's been repeating as we walked together: *We're have to get to where we said we would. We have to get to Logroño, because we said we would get that far.*

"I think we can stop," I say. "I just want to know if that's okay with you. Because," I go on, "tomorrow is going to be like today—pretty in spots, but very much the same kind of prettiness, nothing new, and even hotter, so we'll have to carry more water. I'm worried, frankly, that I can't carry all that we need, and while it's true that I might risk it alone, I won't with you along. And I'm tired," I add, "very tired," inviting her to admit that she is, too.

"We'd get home sooner?" Sarah asks. "We wouldn't stay in Spain as long?"

"Would you like that?"

"Yes." And she says the word again. "Yes."

My husband reacts to the news the same way that everyone will: "What's happened? Is everything all right?"

"Yes. We're just coming home early."

"But why? It's—it's so unlike you." I picture Colin saying this, sitting at our dining room table, the cordless phone pressed to his face.

"I know," I say. "It is."

And I feel how different it is, like a strange taste in my mouth, this sudden ability to change the plan, to change the terms, to *quit*. And not only because I was protecting my daughter, but because I recognized in her the stubborn and expensive pride I've suffered all my life, as much tragic flaw as saving grace.

"Maybe," I say to Colin, "this is my own little pilgrim's progress. The thing I was trying to learn on this stretch of road."

"But," he says, still struggling to understand, to see

us in our little room in the town of Estella, to see our faces and bodies intact. "You are all right? Nothing's happened?"

"Nothing other than I decided—we decided—to cover the last leg on a bus, and come home early."

Monday, July 29, 2002. 11:00 a.m. Estella to Logroño.
Sarah and I look at the same terrain we've seen for three days, hot and sere, wheat and grapes and spiraling dervishes of dust, everything passing us at a rate astonishing to the pedestrians we've become. Little towns beckon from a distance, golden and crenellated, like storybook castles—Azqueta, Luquín, Los Arcos, Torres del Río, Viana. What would have required two punishing days spins past the bus window in a mere hour. Sarah puts her hand on the window, as if to touch their stone walls, remote now, as they weren't a day before.

"So strange," she says, as centuries evaporate in the shimmer of heat hanging over the yellow plain. "So fast."

PART TWO: 1992

One

Fifty kilometers per hour: Leaving the province of
Navarra for Cantabria, of whose road I have walked a
fraction, ten years earlier.

In 1992, seven months pregnant with our son, during a winter leeched of color, a gray season, I arrive in
Burgos in a state of anxious determination. Researching
a novel set in seventeenth-century Spain, I have the
name of a reputable Madrid obstetrician written on a
note folded between bills in my wallet. "You won't need
it," our own doctor promised of this particular piece of
currency, "but it will make you feel better."

As with subsequent journeys to Spain, I begin in
Paris, thereabouts, at Versailles where I refamiliarize

myself with the court of Louis XIV, the Sun King and uncle of my tragic heroine, Marie-Louise de Bourbon, whom he married off to the last Spanish Habsburg, Carlos II. Sacrificed to politics, Marie-Louise traveled, as I travel, backward in time, from France's Enlightenment across the border to Spain's Inquisition. Her husband was impotent; her new people despised her. After failing to produce an heir to the Habsburg throne she was poisoned.

History has preserved nothing of the murdered queen, neither her hopes nor her anguish. At thirty-one, already three years older than Marie-Louise was at the time of her murder, and carrying our second child, a son, I intend to re-create the lost queen, to fill the silence of her death with words—the only solace at my disposal.

After Versailles, I return to Paris to take a night train to Madrid, from which point I will travel on to Burgos to see the cathedral where Marie-Louise and Carlos were to have been married (and to discover the nearby hamlet of Quintanapalla, where the wedding did in fact take place in order to avoid the assassins and sorcerers who might prey upon the superstitious Spanish court).

From Paris to Madrid I share a compartment with two old Spanish women, duennas dressed in black, their heads covered. As we clack into the darkness beyond Paris, two questions preoccupy all of us: Who is to occupy the two bottom bunks? Who must climb into a top one? Together we examine the three tickets we hold and see that it is mine that bears the number of an upper berth. This seems right to me: I am younger not by years but decades. The duennas, however, disapprove. They hand my ticket back and forth to one another, shake their heads. Clearly they consider me too pregnant for even so small an exertion. When I tuck my long skirt around my legs, attempting a modest ascent, they pull me back, one on either arm, scolding. I shrug them off, not intending to be rude—quite the opposite. These grandmothers must sleep in their assigned places, beds into which they can easily slip. To underscore, I point again to the number on my stub, the matching number on the high bed.

But they are obdurate and I succumb, completely, to the authority of years, and of place. Infantilized by sudden tears, far from home and unable to make myself understood, I submit while they turn down the covers, sit me on the narrow bed, and even seize my feet to pull off my shoes. One pushes against my shoulders until I lie down; the other tucks the covers tight over the mound of my belly. Then they sit on the opposite berth and watch me.

All dignity lost, I close my eyes, but cannot dismiss the feel of their kind if disapproving ministrations. Seven years after the death of my mother, who never saw me pregnant, never met the man I married, the father of her grandchildren, the touch of older women is made hot by my bereavement, a touch that surprises me during the impersonal intimacies of a blood pressure reading or a haircut: A woman's hand, how it can burn. Tears leak out from under my closed eyelids, one actually hitting the starched white pillow slip with an audible pop.

"*Gracias,*" I manage, eyes still closed.

The women, at whose faces I cannot bring myself to look, remain seated on the opposite bed. At least, I don't hear them stand. They speak to each other, dialogue punctuated by clucks and the dismissive noise of breath expelled from nostrils, longish silences during which, I am sure, they stare at me, a peculiar blonde woman, a head taller and a lifetime younger. Where am I going, and why am I alone? Why do I weep? Their explanations must be more dire than the truth: that I have the luxury of pursuing a tragedy centuries past, a private passion, while at home in the New World, my husband and daughter await my return.

I stay still on the bed, eyes closed, until I hear them ready themselves for bed and see, through my red lids, that the light has been extinguished.

In Burgos I trail the long dead queen, conjuring scenes with which to fill the blanks of history. At midday I emerge from the grand and Gothic cathedral into the wan winter light. Snowflakes blow horizontally across the gray stones, and the longer I look at the sweeping stairs from the cathedral down to the street the less parallel they appear. I've just visited the tomb of El Cid and the chapel of St. James, the Moor slayer. A little guide, for which I paid a few pesetas, maps out the pilgrim road through Burgos, a road that passes directly before the sanctuary, where for centuries the faithful have come to make obeisance. In the wind, I note the signs for the road, arrows and scallop shells. It's not yet one o'clock, plenty of time to walk a little of this old route. My small suitcase is in a hotel across the River Arlanzon, not far from the train station where I disembarked earlier that day.

I point myself west and soon cross the river again, but not where I'd crossed it before. The water, running swiftly, is a dark gray, and looks gelid and dangerous. Black eelgrass whips below the surface. An hour passes, and now I am beyond the Hospital Del Rey, built in 1195 for ailing pilgrims, supplicants whose journeys ended, in all probability, hundreds of miles short of their hoped-for destination. I cross the river for a third time this day, over the Malatos Bridge, according to the guide. Now I am beyond the border of the city. Now I have walked off my little map. Two o'clock, railroad tracks on my left, the river on my right, I continue west, two kilometers, and then another. What am I doing, trudging away from my suitcase, my passport and my money, all but a few dollars worth?

Ten years later, on the road with my daughter Sarah, I think of this winter day, the white and black birds, the gray landscape, the gray river. A day without color, like an episode of *The Twilight Zone,* a solitary traveler on an unknown road, wearing a coat that no longer buttons, one she holds closed, nearly, with her fists jammed in her pockets. Where am I going in this picture, on this road that I've discovered, twelve centuries old, but new to me?

At three o'clock, at last I return to my senses and turn around to face Burgos, its lights glowing yellow in the early dusk. Beyond the outskirts not only of the city but of myself, I head back with my heart beating so I can hear it, louder, louder, like a story by Poe, frightening me to tears.

"Hormones," I joke later on the phone, watching my reflection in the black windowpane, trying to explain the day to myself as much as to my husband. "I'm pickled in estrogen."

"Maybe you should come home," Colin suggests.

"No, no. I'm fine. It's going very well."

I don't tell him that I've walked until I was exhausted, until I had such strong contractions that I thought I was in labor; that I sat in a courtyard and wept while a woman brought me water and said, each time I tried to stand, *"¡Quédese tranquila! Quédese tranquila!"* and something else that included the word *malo* and which I took to mean it would be bad for the baby if I stood and went on. I don't tell him that it was dark by the time I did get up and retrace my steps to the little hotel; that I was too tired and too unnerved to eat dinner but lay for an hour before calling home, lay very carefully on my bed, the Madrid obstetrician's phone number unfolded on the table beside me; that I stared at the ceiling and practiced being calm.

Walker is born two months later in New York, where we give him a name neither of us consciously connects with the idea of pilgrimage. In fact, though our son is blessed, and equally burdened, with a religious temperament, he doesn't much like to walk. He avoids what he considers inefficient forms of transport.

As for me, infected by my accidental discovery of the road west to Santiago, I promise myself that I will return, and I do.

PART THREE: 1999

One

Sunday, March 21, 1999. 9:00 a.m. Oviedo.

After seven years—seven, that magical cycle: seven
days for a stone boat to cross the seas—I come back to
Spain, leapfrogging ahead on the path, to the province
of León. It is March of 1999. Having been ill and only
recently recovered, my health seems newly valuable,
precious if no longer precarious. It is not the moment,
one might judge, to test it, and Colin is anxious about
my insistence on this trip. What do I want from it, he
wants to know. I can't answer very well. Trying to
explain, I allude to the opening scene of Peter Pan,
when Peter implores Wendy to sew his shadow back
onto his feet. "That's what I want—to walk with

myself and cast a shadow, to walk my way back into my body."

But I don't know, yet, what this means. I've followed only the merest middle fraction of the road west of Burgos, infinitesimal, but enough, like a dormant germ, to lie in wait and then, abruptly, burgeon and take hold.

So here I am in an airport in Oviedo, carrying too many maps, too many history books, a surfeit of guides. Not enough socks, a rucksack that fits poorly, and one weak knee, but these are discoveries I've yet to make.

At Oviedo's bus station bar, I'm drinking *café con leche* as I wait for my bus to Astorga, the point at which I'll begin the 283 kilometers that will deliver me to Santiago. Overhead, an outsized television plays nine channels at once, its screen divided like a game of tic-tac-toe: newsreel footage of World War II; a golf tournament; a nature program—predator and prey; an aerobics class; a documentary on ancient Chinese burial practices; CNN, etc. There is no linear time, the animate eye of the TV insists; it's all happening at once. Patrons drink, smoke, wait to depart. Next to me at the bar, a woman plays a handheld computer game of solitaire, her legs crossed, one foot swinging. Exhausted by the loss of a night's sleep and agitated by the electronic blips of the solitaire, I feel a shiver of disorientation. It's as if a trapdoor has opened under my bar stool and, in the manner of a cartoon character, I'm suspended in space, conscious that I am about to plummet.

By the time I get to Astorga I'm more optimistic, reassured by the discovery that the road is marked far more clearly than I had imagined, or even hoped. Yellow scallop shells and arrows make losing one's way seem impossible. It is three o'clock in the afternoon, the hour when I should be finding a room, ensuring a good night's sleep before the first leg of my long walk, but already I've squandered whole days as a passenger, strapped in my seat on two planes and two buses, suffering boredom and leg cramps and spasms of claustrophobia. I must be tired, but I feel too restless to wait for morning to begin, and so, in defiance of all I've read in the guides, I set out.

The path runs along a cement sidewalk and then veers off into a dirt track, twisting away from the city past houses and dripping green yards. This is easy, nothing to this test I've set for myself, one foot in front of another, but I'm aware of my heartbeat quickening with anxiety as well as exertion. I am nowhere, nowhere I know, and the sun is setting. A few kilometers after the hamlet of Valdeviejas, I come upon a tree hung with mirrors. It is dusk, purple edged with black, and the mirrors twist and flash light. A way to scare off birds, I tell myself, to protect fruit, and yet the tree is terrifying, like some sort of occult sentinel.

I can make out headlamps traveling along the N-VI, the route for pilgrims in cars, and strike off in that direction. What could have possessed me to set out into imminent darkness toward a sinking sun? A highway will offer places to spend the night, I tell myself, willing myself to forget what I know of roads made for cars: One hundred kilometers can pass without offering refuge. Without reflective clothing, I cannot walk on the shoulder, and several times I stumble, once somersaulting into a wet ditch, where I lie cursing myself for being so impulsive—stupid—as to head west into the shadows, without knowing where I might find a place to sleep and wait for the light. But I am on a road, with money in my pocket, the vision of the mirror-hung tree impelling me forward. I'll land somewhere.

Hostal Restaurante Las Palmeras, in fact, where the proprietor regards me with suspicion. Dirty and wild-eyed, I'm far off the pilgrim track that offers a steady stream of ragged travelers. "Twenty-five hundred pesetas," he says, and seeing my incomprehension, he writes the number on a piece of paper. I give him the bills, and he hands me a key marked 209, which gives entrée to a tiny room and bath, outfitted with scratchy sheets and rough towels. I lock the door and pull the curtains on the night, the night hung with mirrors.

Monday, March 22, 1999. 7:00 a.m. A roadside inn.
Morning at last, after a night that disappears, eight hours of sleep that feel less like something than nothing, a jump cut. How I hate when that happens; it strikes me as a theft. Somewhere, deep inside myself, I was dreaming—and I missed it. But at least it isn't Sunday anymore, and for this I'm grateful, that day having never lost the melancholy of my schoolgirl's attempt to reach God, to sit in a pew, patient, penitent, helpless. Will God arrive? Will God announce Himself?

Is this a reason for my walk, I wonder, drinking my coffee at the bar among the boisterous truck drivers. I find it hard to wait—to hope—in faith, whether that faith be in God, or in providence, or in enlightenment. I would rather walk toward it. Earn it. Suffer for it.

Overtake it.

By 9:30 a.m. I am near Santa Catalina de Somoza. It's cold—my breath comes in white plumes—but I've been walking too briskly to feel chilled. I pass an old factory, fallen into disrepair and taken over by storks. Huge nests, like black boats, wide and deep, balance on the ruined roofs. The birds stand along naked beams like guards, motionless in their vigilance. The scene is beautiful, and unnerving. Cows graze below. I hear the herd before I see the animals, bells hung around their necks ringing as they move their heads to eat. A giant wind chime, I think before I see them. The pastures in March are an intense green I associate with Ireland. I can't quite believe this green under my feet, green splashed with white and purple flowers.

Just west of Vega de Valcarce, an old man sits on a pasture fence, ensnaring me in one of the half-signed inarticulate dialogues that will come to characterize my passage through Spain.

"Are you all alone?" the exchange always begins. *¿Sola? Completamente sola?*

"*Sí.*"

"*¿Por qué?*"

I shrug. Why not, I learn to ask. *¿Por qué no?*

"Where are you going?"

"*A Santiago.*"

He nods. "Ah," he says. The destination explains everything and anything. After all, solitude may be my chosen, my deserved, penance.

You don't have to carry your water, he lets me know, shaking his head at my filled liter bottle. The water the cows drink is good.

"Thank you," I say. Lacking words, the medium on which I depend, I execute a respectful little gesture of good-bye, something like the curtsy I made each morning to the headmistress of my elementary school. Without a skirt, I pluck at the air, then smile, wave, and walk on, wondering at myself.

"*Se vende miel*—Honey for sale." The signs recur along the road, apiaries often set up on platforms of stone offered by the ruins of an otherwise abandoned building. The hives are silent and still, but curiously they convey a kind of heat and purpose—perhaps by virtue of what I imagine inside: the congestion of workers creating and filling cells, the genius of symmetry filled with gold. I stop to watch as bees leak from one round white hive, like steam curling from under a lid.

"*Buenos días*," I say to an old couple I pass. They are sitting on a low stone wall, arms crossed, silent and staring, a common sight, but the calm of these encounters still disturbs me, used as I am to elderly Americans watching a television screen, disguising what is in rural Spain a more naked passage of time, of life. Mortality.

"Buenos días is 'good morning,'" the man replies. "*Buenas tardes* is 'good afternoon.'" He shows me his watch. "Four on the clock," he says in his heavy accent. The woman asks the obligatory question.

"*¿Solita?*"

I nod without stopping, "*Sí.*"

She shakes her head disapprovingly, and I wave with what I hope seems like pluck rather than defiance, and continue walking west. The man—her husband I assume—gets up to follow, and his dog stands, too. I struggle against my irritation. I don't want this officious companion, not even for a kilometer or two.

"England or America?" he demands, pointing at my chest.

"America."

He rubs his hands together, conveying delight. "Me, I have a friend in Chicago."

"New York," I reply. He rubs his hands again, with even more gusto.

"That's good, no?"

I make the universal gesture of ambivalence: the head wag of yes and no, *comme ci comme ça*, and turn up my empty palms. You tell me, the motion says to him, and he answers, "Yes!"

After ten minutes or so, I stop wondering when he's going to drop back and bid me good-bye, and I stop walking so fast. My companion, a "gentleman tailor," as he describes himself, is twice my age, bent and wheezing, his relative infirmity a gift, because, as it turns out, when I slow down I see more of what surrounds me, hamlets that might be two or even six hundred years old, stone houses with livestock on the ground floor, white curtains blowing out from the windows above, lanes filled with dogs and chickens and cows and cats. A man splits firewood with an ax; a woman breaks clods of earth with her hoe. The only indication that we all inhabit the same century is the occasional phone wire that penetrates a rooftop, the bright red shine of a car parked in a barn.

Afraid of falling behind the pace I'd set for myself, I had been marching resolutely forward, bent on reaching the day's destination, and the white-haired tailor strikes me as a little messenger from God, especially when he tells me that O Cebreiro is only eight kilometers away. I'd thought twenty, and was afraid I'd never make it by nightfall.

"We will walk there together," he announces, and he names the little towns through which we'll pass.

"¿Solita?" he asks again as we walk, and he returns to the question, pointing at my chest. "Yes," I say, each time. "I'm alone." And each time he nods, but not with censure. "Bachelor," he says of himself.

At La Faba, he stops at a gate and rings a bell, summoning an old woman who opens a garage door, behind which is a bar set up on a cold concrete floor. *"¡Cerveza!"* The tailor wants a beer, and he wants me to drink one with him. Crestfallen when I refuse, he turns his back on me to talk to the woman, leaving me like a child in the company of only his dog, whose ears and tail have been docked without any attempt at grace or even tidiness. Cut crookedly in half, the ears don't match, and the hindquarters convey nothing so much as amputation, sacrifice, wagging a hopeful three inches of neither stump nor tail. After a minute, he sees a cat and takes off, and I pace in the doorway, trying to hurry my companion.

A few kilometers on, the tailor asks a question. "How do you say ———?" he begins, and he fills in the blank with a gesture, threading the first finger of one hand through a circle formed by the thumb and forefinger of the opposite.

"I don't know," I tell him. "I don't understand," and he repeats the gesture, but closer to me, just inches from my crotch.

Surely he can't mean intercourse. I'm frightened for a moment, then amused. Can this be the subtext of his many announcements that he's a bachelor? I point to my wedding ring. "No," I say. "No."

He smiles and shrugs. "Do you blame me for trying?" the gesture conveys. I remind myself how often we have stopped for him to catch his breath, that he's told me of his parents' deaths—*infarto* and *tromboso*—words spoken in the dramatic and respectful tones reserved for gods and fates. If need be I could easily outrun him, or push him over the hill we are ascending.

"No," I say one more time, and I tell him I love my husband, or that my husband is my lover. *"Mi esposo es mi amor."* I find it mysterious how many Spanish words I can retrieve, scattered fragments from long-past trips to Mexico, for I have never studied the language.

Another kilometer passes; we ascend another hill. My companion points out the scenery. "Camera! Camera!" he insists, aggrieved and even incredulous when I tell him I have no camera with me. I am not going to take any pictures but keep all I see in my head. I point to my temple, and he makes a *Bah!* sort of gesture, swatting at such foolishness. But I know I am right. I can imagine the snapshots, their smallness that would deny the majesty of the sky and hills, the colors off, grays missing their purple, greens dull and ordinary. O Cebreiro is at the peak, a mountain pass linking the province of León and the region of Galicia. The gentleman tailor stops to catch his breath. "How do you say," he says after a moment, and I prepare myself for another awkward advance, *"¿titas?"*

"No comprendo," I say, playing dumb as a first strategy. He repeats the word, reaching out as if to touch my breasts.

"No!" I say, pushing his hands away. "Come on!" The tailor laughs. It has become a joke, his predation, by virtue of my youth and strength, my ability to escape or even punish.

He looks at his wristwatch. "Six on the clock," he says, and then he warns me that between us and the still invisible town of O Cebreiro are owls, bats, and something else that comes out as night falls. "*Lobos*," he says again to emphasize, and, I imagine, to convince me of the value of his walking by my side, but no, "It is time I go home," he concludes.

He asks, in words and pantomime, for writing materials, and I hand him my journal, in which he's seen me make notes, and a pen. "Here," I say, opening it to the last page, so as not to interrupt my entries. The old man sits down on the ground, legs crossed as in a fairy-tale illustration of a tailor. He bends over in concentration, producing a few slow strings of letters with exaggerated tails and flourishes: a penmanship that bears witness to the value of literacy, and attests to how infrequently this man engages in the act of writing. He hands the composition book back to me and holds out his hand so that I may pull him to his feet.

Together we consider his work. *Amigos del Camino de Santiago*, I make out, the uppercase *A* and *C* and *S* enhanced with extra loops and points, and the name of the town where we met, and where he must live, Herrerias de Valcarcel, and the province, León. Below it is his signature and the date: a document that testifies to our brief time together.

I hold out my hand, and he takes it. "Friends of the road," I translate his words, and we both nod as we shake hands, suddenly formal and awkward.

I watch as he descends the track, moving faster now that gravity is on his side, now that shadows gather and wolves prowl.

How strange this is, how fearsomely beautiful. Snow begins to fall around me as I walk, as I hurry up the steepening hill. Spinning flakes catch the day's last light, glitter on the thorny brush, and on the pale stones below my feet, their purple shadows. This can't be the first lonely walk I've taken, not the first empty road I've followed, and yet I have never felt my solitude so keenly. "No one," I think as I climb, searching for the next shadowed bend in the track, the first sight of the town. There is no one in sight, and much as I try to stop hearing them, my footfalls repeat the syllables, *no one, no one.* The dark descends theatrically, inspiring visions of a Red Riding Hood wolf, walking upright and speaking the language of men. Out from behind a boulder or a tree he springs, lecturing before devouring me. "Foolish girl," he scolds, "who walks through woods alone." Inside him, squashed against the hot red walls of his lungs and heart, I meet my grandmother, a woman who was easy prey for no creature.

The moon has risen, nearly full. Under its light the night is vast and absolute, the night of nothingness, of annihilation. Wolves: How alive the idea makes me feel, hurrying toward safety, quivering in my own flesh, almost running now under my heavy pack, feet sliding on loose gravel and stones, eyes stinging with snow. The moon has done this: changed the road from gray to silver, carried me from day to magic morbid night. He lied, the lecherous tailor. It was never eight kilometers, and the price for rebuffing him will be—what? Shadows bloom with teeth and tongues and slaver; the shining road is ever steeper; inside my clothes I'm wet with fear, and my thoughts have collapsed into the flat recitations of the doomed. It will be over quickly, I tell myself, not like my mother's cancer or my grandmother's failing heart, not like dying by degrees of despair.

Abruptly the dirt track meets paving stones and I am in a tiny and ethereal hamlet, a village seemingly untouched for centuries, medieval stone structures with round thatched roofs, pointed like witches' hats. Windows splash gold squares of light on the snowy ground. I've reached an altitude where the snows haven't melted, where cars haven't climbed. Three wires, like those of a puppet master, penetrate the roof of one building, and after looking around myself I head in that direction. There are no signs posted, but the guides mention an inn in O Cebreiro, and phone wires seem as good an announcement as any. But before I've walked ten paces, a man in a heavy coat crosses my path. He looks me up and down. *"¿Posada?"* he asks. *"¿Refugio?"*

"Posada," I say, choosing hotel over pilgrim refuge, silence rather than the obligation to share tales of the road. He nods and confirms me in the direction I was walking, pointing toward the building with three wires.

Only one room left, and it is mine. How often will this be true, my luck that feels like grace, like God was there all along, holding off the wolves and saving my bed? The inn looks like a convent. My cell-like room has a tiny window with a single wooden shutter, white-washed walls adorned by a single crucifix, a bathtub the size of a laundry sink, with a shard of soap and a rough towel. But the water is blessedly hot, and grime rolls off me, turning the white suds gray.

Downstairs, the refectory is furnished by two trestle tables, on whose benches a few people linger, silhouettes before the orange fire, which pops and spits so loudly that it outtalks their murmured conversation. A woman wearing an apron brings me a bowl of soup, a spoon, and a basket of bread. "Gracias," I say, the only word that passes between us, and she nods, barely. I've fallen through one fairy tale into another: escaped the wolf's jaws and landed in the beast's castle, where enchanted tables set themselves. From a carafe in the center of the table, hands pour a mug of red wine and leave it at my side. I feel ridiculous, a child rescued from nightmares. My cheeks burn with wind and snow, hot water and red wine. Will each day be like this, a morality play, rehearsals of death, and abrupt gifts of resurrection? I hope so, for isn't that why I came?

Two

Tuesday, March 23, 1999. 7:00 a.m. O Cebreiro.
I wake to a square of light laid, like an extra blanket, over the white bedclothes. Downstairs, I eat alone again, and in silence. Mug and plate appear with enchanted speed, perpetuating the spell I expected to be broken by a good night's sleep. Two pitchers, one with black coffee, the other with hot milk, and slices of bread almost too thick to bite, saturated with local honey, dark and flecked, with a complex flavor, almost as if it had been smoked. I eat more than I want, trying to taste it consciously, trying to commit something so ephemeral as a mouthful of honey to memory.

Outside it is cold and aggressively clear—all that I see is tightened into a focus that makes me feel smudged and soft by comparison. Light sparks off ice-rimed eaves and cobbles. I am wearing all my clothes. Thermal long johns under my jeans, T-shirt, turtleneck, sweater and jacket on top with an extra two pairs of socks, rolled as padding under my pack's shoulder straps, which, I noted in my cell's tiny mirror, have left a matched set of bruises over my collarbones.

For three hours, or about fifteen kilometers, the road aligns itself with that used by farmers and local residents, but at the town of Biduedo it veers away into a narrow dirt footpath. Now the road is a pilgrim way and nothing more; for centuries, the only people to have walked it are those en route to Santiago.

In Ramil, hungry, I stop outside a restaurant, one with a menu posted and translated into French and English and German. Inside, tables are filled with pilgrims, whose bicycles lie in a tangled heap by the entrance. Through the window I see them laughing and singing and playing table soccer, and turn away from the noise, the threat of inclusion. For five hours I've carried the silence of the refectory at O Cebreiro, and I dread the obligatory recitations among the pilgrims, who we are and where we come from, what we do and why we're walking. Each time I feel less able to answer even one of these questions with certainty, and so I tease myself along with a few handfuls of trail mix and a carton of apricot nectar.

Another hour passes and I am in Triacastela whose churchyard I enter, stepping among the headstones. Some of these are grand and include red stained glass through which the sun passes, splashing bloodstains on the bare earth between plots. Inside the sanctuary, there are no effigies before which I can kneel, no candles to light, nothing on which to squander a few more pesetas. A table near the altar holds a stamp and ink pad, and as I lack the official pilgrim passport, I use them to impress a memento of my trespass on one page of my journal. The vestments room, where hang the priest's surplice and stole, is open, door ajar, and I go in. A table spread with a white cloth offers things I could easily take: a tray bearing cruets for water and wine, a scallop shell, a salver. The most beautiful object is a small hinged wood chest holding a vial of chrism, the oil with which the priest anoints the dying. I pick it up and smell the oil. How I want this box. I consider theft, or purchase—I could leave more money than it is worth— but each seems equally wrong, for either leaves the priest empty-handed, the dying bereft. Why do I want it so? To assuage my sense of mortality, to everyday anoint my able-bodied self? For years I've been my own priest, ever since, during the course of a long-overdue Lenten confession, I told the pastor of our Brooklyn diocese that I was married to a Quaker and with him had two unbaptized children. "Well," he said, "I can't absolve you of that. If that's true, you're not a Catholic."

"What would I have to do, to be accepted back into the church?" I asked, irritated by the discourse, which seemed to me to address none of my sins, a topic at which we hadn't yet arrived.

His answer—to catechize and then remarry my Quaker husband—inspired apostasy rather than reform. I use the local church for my solitary prayers, avoid Mass but still push open the heavy door to walk between the aisles of empty pews and kneel at the unlit altar. Like someone about to wash her face, I plunge both hands into the font and splash holy water over my head and neck. Sometimes, I catch the end of an Easter service, slipping in line to receive the Eucharist, opening my mouth to the hand of the priest, aware of the awkward intimacy—a stranger's fingers laying bread on my tongue. But mostly I am alone in church, comfortable in my excommunication.

I push my forefinger deep into the reservoir of oil and encounter something soft and fibrous: a wad of cotton. A few filaments cling to my nail as I withdraw the finger, anoint my throat, my head, my heart.

The box, which I desire, and which would be so easy to take, I leave on the table. There will be moments in years to come when I remember it, when I can close my eyes, conjure it exactly, and feel an undiminished longing.

It's three o'clock before I stop for what will become my favorite snack on the road, two cafés con leche grandes and a saucer of *magdalenas*, or madeleines, their flavor unremarkable compared to their associative power. Always alert to encounters with symbols, I bite into the first cake carefully, almost furtively, as if wary of its possible effects. I've never before eaten a madeleine. Will the past come rushing back?

Oddly, on this road the past has returned—nothing to do with a cake, of course, but the unaccustomed days of solitude, body occupied, mind freed, and the linear, implicitly narrative aspect of a walk from here to there. Not that I hadn't expected the past, but I imagined it would arrive in the form of reckoning—pictured myself as a moral auditor, determined to go over the books and balance things up, see where payment was yet due. What might have transpired that didn't demand examination, adjustment?

Of course, I pictured the setting for this private auto-da-fé all wrong. Having been to southern Spain during the dry month of August, its sere fields rustling under furnace winds, and to Burgos and Avila during dead gray winter, I imagined the country's northwest would be a similarly punitive environment. Instead, I find Galicia lush, even jarringly lovely. The water of melting snow gathers into countless streams, and I walk each day to the sound of water, a forgiving noise. Listening to it, I remember conversations from my childhood, dialogues that unfolded between adults, frustrating in their opacity. Now, mysteriously, they are available to me, as if replayed to my adult and knowing ears.

After years of parsing each gesture and phrase for its burden of meaning—just whose fault was it when things went so wrong?—I felt, before this trip, that I was on the verge of understanding the complex of culpability that was my family. Walking along, I can almost see it in the landscape before me, imposed over the sheep and the pastures, transparent like a cutaway diagram of a vast and sinister factory, with countless cubicles and a thousand tiny rooms, a way to record and file it all. I stop for a moment to consider this: my insistent pursuit of judgment, of judging us all. What have I learned from this exhausting effort? How have

noise they stop moving to consider its source. Then they run, gobbling furiously together and flapping their clumsy little wings.

My knee hurts; it definitely hurts. Admitting this to myself isn't the defeat I expected. Somehow it allows me to relax. I sit on the wall, swinging my leg gingerly and feeling the creak in the joint. Christian Science, the faith in which I was thoroughly indoctrinated between the ages of two and ten, was a system of magnificent denial, one I mastered occasionally to will away pain or illness. These few successes made all the failures that much more humiliating. Feeling my knee, deciding not to resist it, I realize that I've always understood transcendence as proceeding from denial. What if it comes through its opposite, acceptance?

I pass through Lavandeira, a tiny village that for some reason I expected would be a little hub of commerce, with a store where I could buy an Ace bandage, a bar with café con leche, a phone to call home before the kids go to school. The force of desire, I guess, its power to direct what we believe.

Two o'clock and I'm at Brea, another tiny town, noteworthy for its signpost that reads *"100 km a Santiago."* Three girls with backpacks approach me, cameras held out, and I take their pictures as they pose next to the sign. One offers, in heavily accented English, to take my picture and send it to me. "You write," she says. "You write the address," but I shake my head. "No," I say, "No thank you. I don't need one."

Brea's other feature of interest is a rabbit farm, like those I've seen for chickens, hundreds of white rabbits in a huge concrete structure, smelling far worse than pigs or goats or cows or anything I've ever smelled before. Perhaps it's just the incongruity of the stench emanating from such magically white animals. Why doesn't their fur get stained when they are packed together so vilely? I walk on but can't get the picture of the rabbit barracks out of my head, imagining the ranks of black-suited magicians that might require so many white rabbits, or, worse, all the little feet chopped off and dyed to make colored charms for luck.

The three girls and I pass and overtake each other, back and forth, all of us limping, I note with a certain smugness, having concluded that I'm a good fifteen years older than they. But I'm not smug for long, the maps say I'm barely halfway through today's twenty-two kilometers. At the village of Ferreiros—meaning "blacksmiths," upon whom pilgrims relied to shoe their horses and hobnail their boots—I find what I've been looking for: a bar with a public phone box, and I call home, talking to the children for nearly twenty minutes, pouring all the coins I have into the slot: 2,292 pesetas, or sixteen dollars—cheap for the satisfaction they buy. What did you eat for breakfast? Cheerios? What game did you play? What book did you read? Is your room a mess, or is it tidy? We tumble through unnecessary questions, so I can listen to the sound of their disembodied voices, always higher, more piping than in person, making them seem younger, more vulnerable than the image I hold of them. "Quick, put Daddy on," I say as I drop my last coins into the phone, and Colin comes on the line for the last minute or two, and we have a different but still essentially contentless exchange, a message that might be transmitted in an instant: We're here, both of us, alive and well if many miles apart, and yet we have to maintain this connection for as long as we can. I have to spend every last coin and let the time run out.

I hang up and stare, caught in the limbo between here and there, between this walk, this passage—this time out of time—and my real life, my work and my family. A man approaches, holding out a cigarette, a remedy for whatever ails the staring woman. I start to say no, but then change my mind and accept the cigarette. How pleasant it might be, the tiny transgression, if saved for one of those picturesque slate walls, bars of gold sun slanting onto the green fields. He offers a light and I shake my head. "Gracias," I say, placing the cigarette carefully between the pages of my journal, where it won't break.

He tears a few matches from his book and gives those to me as well. "*Vaya con Dios,*" he says.

"¡Gracias!" I say again, "¡Gracias!" and I wring his hand as if he's given me a gift of great value, which I feel he has.

Now that I am within a hundred kilometers—four days of walking—from Santiago, more and more people I encounter call out greetings, mostly Vaya con Dios and a similar phrase that I haven't heard before, *Vaya con fé,* a bit less presumptuous and more pleasing.

Four kilometers outside of Portomarín I find the wall for which I've been saving my cigarette, and light it with one of the matches struck against a rough stone. The tobacco makes me dizzy, a kind of sweet reeling perfumed dizziness, not at all unpleasant. Gold slats of sun poke through the trees, and there are flowers, too: tiny purple violets and bigger yellow blooms that look like pansies, and huge umbels of Queen Anne's lace, as gorgeous and astounding as they are commonplace. Chunks of granite heave up through the grass, and the air is mild. I lie on the wall with my feet on a tree trunk, keeping my knee up for a full ten minutes, until five o'clock. This day has provided many little object lessons in pain and how it's related to anxiety. While I was worrying about finding a phone to call my children before they left for school, chiding myself for not calling the previous evening, my knee ached much more intensely than it did after I hung up, when for an hour or more it didn't hurt at all. Perhaps this has something to do with how I metabolize ibuprofen, but I don't think so. When I'm calm the pain seems actually smaller. When I worry about it, it grows, threatening to engulf the whole experience of walking.

So many farmers in the region keep bees that their buzzing is constant, at times nerve-wracking, but as I climb down from the wall it pulses and soothes, like a mantra. By six I can see the River Mino, and the two cities of Portomarín, the remains of the medieval town nearly submerged in the river and a subsequent incarnation built higher on the river's north bank. I stop midway across the bridge to look down at the submarine walls. The surface of the river appears calm, but below, long green weeds ripple in the current, and the crumbling walls below seem to sway and dance. How is it that ruins underwater have such power? The vision of fish swimming through doors changes the doors, removes them to a realm of myth rather than simple mortality: transformation instead of decay.

The bridge leads into a road that might not seem so steep were it not for the pack, the knee, the hour.

But when I reach the central plaza, everything I want is there: pharmacy, hotel, restaurant, and cathedral, whose doors blow suddenly open with a blast of organ music. A spray of delicate birds scatter, black against the pale stone walls, like music notes ascending. It is the Wednesday before Palm Sunday, and around every corner come silent streams of women wearing black, their heads covered modestly in nets of lace. I follow them, helpless to resist such unexpected beauty, step through the arched stone portal of the Church of San Nicolas and into the twinkling dark of the sanctuary, the nave's deep shadows offset by chapels bright with votive candles.

I stand and sit and genuflect along with the rest of the congregation, excused from listening to words I don't understand even as I follow the familiar forms of the service, whispering what I remember of the English liturgy. The priest is thorough in his perfuming of the altar; he fills the censer and swings it vigorously, dispensing stinging clouds of incense, so thick that for a moment the crucifix behind the altar disappears and those in the front pews sneeze and cough. Conspicuous in my grimy clothes, I wait my turn for the priest's hand bearing the Host and, as I am clearly a pilgrim, receive his benediction as well. Briefly he lets his hand rest on my bare head and murmurs a prayer I cannot translate.

Kneeling back in my pew, I can't explain my tears any more than I can stop them.

After dinner at the Posada de Portomarín, where my room overlooks the plaza and cathedral, I sort and wash my socks and underpants, all but one pair of each, which I leave dry for tomorrow. I soak everything in hot water and use an entire little cake of Maya soap, the brand with the flamenco dancer on the black wrapper—an old favorite of my mother's, one it's been years, decades, since I've smelled. I slip the wrapper between two leaves of my journal. After a third lathering the water finally runs down the drain clear, and I wring out the socks and underwear, roll them in the bath towel, and step on them to press the moisture out.

These rituals of hygiene give me a pleasure beyond the satisfaction of my not having to pack and carry dirty underclothes tomorrow. The meditative quality of the pilgrimage is enhanced by performing these small and solitary chores. A hotel laundry service could do a better job, return the garments soft from having been tumbled in a dryer, but I haven't the time for that, and scrubbing out the dirt that, step by step, I ground into the socks completes a circle, offering a fragment of what feels like knowing, if not knowledge. I think of our cat, inside for the evening and sitting in her favorite chair to wash each paw thoroughly, her head dipping rhythmically, her eyes narrow with pleasure.

Thursday, March 25, 1999. 9:00 a.m. Portomarín
At breakfast, the hotel restaurant is taken over by a high school group, table after table crammed with uniformed girls and boys, and I'm grateful for the excuse to have café con leche and madeleines at the bar, where I feel less conspicuous eating alone. The de rigeur television hangs from a ceiling bracket, and overhead a movie plays, some kind of bad girl adventure featuring convertible car chases and beach parties with throngs of frantic teens dancing in bikinis. The energy on the screen underscores how depleted I feel, sore and deeply weary, and ridiculously discouraged by the fact that none of my clothes are dry, not the ones I laundered, nor any of the rest. I left the window open as I slept, and it must have rained for hours. When I woke, damp air filled the room, and even my blankets were covered with fine droplets.

I buy an Ace-type bandage—*elástica fuerte*—and wrap my knee, which does seem to help, but in truth, on this fifth day my legs are so sore all over that it's hard to pick out any individual pain, which is almost a mercy.

Once I'm beyond the town, it begins to rain again, not hard but a steady gray, soporific rain, hissing through the pine needles, pattering on leaves. I'd be overcome by the desire to lie down, were it not for the slugs. Black and leathery, they are far bigger than any I've seen before. As much as five inches long, they crisscross the path, decorating it with their crooked iridescent trails.

What I hadn't foreseen about my plastic poncho is how noisy it is. Rain patters on the hood and makes a punitive slapping sound. When it's properly fastened, snapped under the chin so that it doesn't blow back, the hood blinkers me. Because I can't see to either side walking is reduced to a forward trudge into the rain. Several times I stop to take it off, but then I end up putting it back on because I'm cold.

By one it's stopped raining, or perhaps I've walked out from under the clouds. I find a wall dry enough to sit on, and unpack the food I've brought, bread and jam and sunflower seeds, a carton of apricot nectar. It's oddly quiet here, just outside of Castromayor, a deeply green and vegetative quiet that makes thinking seem useless, a waste of energy. I have an unfamiliar sense of emptiness, like an overturned cup, neither pleasant nor unpleasant. I sit on the wall in my wet clothes, nearly warm when the sun comes out. Stretched along the dirt track is an odd sight, one that will be repeated over the coming kilometers: a train of black fuzzy caterpillars, hitched one to another. I count thirty-one of them, not moving, but seemingly stuck together. Is it sexual, the exchange of semen or some other fluid? Is it to deter predators by together appearing to be bigger than a snack? I watch for a while, but they don't move.

By 2:30 p.m. I've reached Ligonde, where I phone home from an outdoor kiosk, a quick call because the connection is bad, and the weather abruptly worse. Sleet blows sideways in blasts of undiluted misery, changing directions, stinging my eyes and my cheeks, whipping my poncho around, picking up its hem and slapping me in the face. When a group of six pilgrims push their bicycles past me, I follow them. The scallop shells hanging from their handlebars seem like enough of a guarantee that we share a destination, and they're much easier to see than the way markers. After an hour they stop at a wayside tavern—"*Welcome, Bienvenue, Willkommen Pelegrinos*" reads a battered tiny sign over the door—and I stop as well; we enter the dank and grubby house en masse.

Sixteen people huddle around a long trestle table, conversing in French mostly, although everyone seems to lapse into their own tongues without regard to his or her listener's ability to understand. Our hostess, in her seventies, pours coffee from an enamel pot into chipped yellow mugs, terrible coffee that manages to be both weak and bitter. But it's hot; we take heaping spoons of sugar from the communal bowl and milk from the pitcher; we drain our cups and hold them out for more; cut slabs from the big, lumpy loaf of bread on the board and spread them with butter and dark honey, a comfortingly infantile experience, returning me to a red plastic kindergarten chair, waiting my turn to reach into the cracker basket as it passed from child to child.

Outside, the weather remains wild, and everyone lingers at the long sticky table, trading advice and information in mangled French. One of the cyclists tells me that soon we will reach Alto do Rosario, where, if the weather improves, we will be able to see the Pico Sacro or "sacred mountain" near Santiago, up which the mythic queen Lupa sent the disciples when they were looking for a fitting place to bury the remains of St. James. Traditionally the vantage has been a place to stop and pray the rosary, or at least pause and meditate, but on this wet and windy afternoon I arrive in Palas de Rei having never seen Alto do Rosario, or much of the road before me. I've covered nearly twenty-five kilometers, but it's only five o'clock, and it's quite light, lighter than it has been all day, and the evening looms. The idea of checking into a little room seems unbearable, claustrophobic, so despite misgivings, I continue walking—crazy, totally crazy, I keep telling myself. None of my guides indicate that there will be any accommodations between Palas and Melide, a good fifteen kilometers away. But I'm helpless to stop myself.

East of Palas de Rei, the road becomes a path and the path sinks into the ground until I am traveling through a trench. It's stopped raining, but the air remains damp and my saturated clothes don't dry at all. Still, I'm grateful not to have to keep my hood up, and as long as I keep moving it's warm, if steamy, under the plastic poncho. As I walk I run my fingers along the moss that grows up the sides of what might be mistaken for a riverbed, centuries of pilgrims having washed through, carving the path so deep that I can't see the sights I pass, not the twelfth-century Romanesque Church of San Julian do Camino, not the Castle of Pambre.

Why do I like this road? Why do I love it? What can be the comfort of understanding my footprint as just one among the millions? Each day I tire myself to the point that I am indifferent to what tourists seek, shops and sights and restaurants and galleries, morsels of an alien culture, toothsome and purchasable. All I want is what my feet deliver: simultaneous communion with those dead and those yet to be, walking myself, step by step, lower lower, into a deeper consciousness of mortality, each life unbearably small, impossibly brief, while time and history flood ever backward and forward. Off the path, back home in my usual life, the contemplation of this truth grieves and oppresses me, but while I'm walking it's quite the opposite; I feel myself alive; I feel my small life burning brightly. That it will be extinguished seems right and even beautiful to me. What would I be worth, were I to have myself forever?

At arm's length the moss under my fingertips looks as if it would feel like velvet, a brilliant gemlike green, smooth as Chartreuse liqueur. But it's rough to the touch, almost abrasive, and when I pause to inspect it, the seemingly uniform green breaks down into a range of hues, from nearly yellow to emerald. I draw close enough that my nose grazes the dense nap of minuscule frond-like leaves. Having stopped to look, it's hard to pull my eyes away.

I emerge west of Disicabo—west of nowhere—and come upon a hotel in a clearing, an unlikely location for a hotel, but it seems somehow apt that I might arise from the ground, from deep thoughts, and find rest immediately, without having to search for it. I ring the bell and wait, cupping my hands to peer through the window by the front door. No one answers, and the lobby is empty.

A vase of fresh (or are they artificial?) flowers sits on the desk; a newspaper lies untouched on a low glass table set between two club chairs; blue and yellow flames tongue an artificial log on the hearth. I watch them, my forehead resting on the cool windowpane, as I press the lighted button and listen for a third time to the shrill tone of the electric bell. What a peculiar hotel this is, flanked by an empty parking lot and seeming very un-Spanish, as if it were lifted from the perimeter of a midwestern highway and dropped into this alien landscape. It's six kilometers to Melide, an hour of walking past dusk, but no one is answering the bell, and I tell myself how inauspicious a sign is the gas log, with its warmthless blue flames.

I turn down the marked path, which cuts away from the asphalt road into some woods. A field opens ahead, and from it I hear an odd huffing noise, one made, I guess, by a cow. I picture the animal's wide wet nose, her cavernous nostrils pressed into a tuft of grass, exhaling in gusts, but when I look for her what I find is a man, and he's masturbating. Not in a secluded corner, not camouflaged by trees or shrubs or hayrick, instead he stands smack in the middle of a lushly green field studded all over with violets. He sees me see him, but he doesn't stop, he doesn't fasten his pants and disappear. Frightened, I begin to walk more quickly, because walking seems safer somehow than running, which might be construed as an accusation, but I'm heading toward dense woods on both sides of the path, and rationalizations aside, my knees hurt too much to run, let alone outrun anyone, and my pack is heavy, my clothing wet—there are any number of reasons why I would not be able to escape this man, tall, heavy, and muscular. I remind myself that exhibition-ists are not generally considered violent or likely to rape. But still.

I retrace my steps, quickly, and he sees me and I see him see me. We enact a bizarre little choreography of he and I heading first this way, then that, and it's impossi-ble for me to know if he's frightened and trying to get away or predatory and planning to pounce. Then the two of us are moving east, he on the woods side of the field, I on the road side, neither of us drawing ahead or falling behind, neither entering the green limbo between. As for me, panicked, I pray for a car to come along the deserted stretch of asphalt, anyone I might flag down and beg a ride to Melide, but only a single truck passes, the driver in the cab high up and remote, the truck going too fast for him to see a woman waving from the shoulder, a woman dressed in dark clothes and walking in a dark landscape.

Because the man is walking with his penis still

exposed, held in his hand, I keep my own eyes trained on the ground before me, keeping him enough in my peripheral vision to see if he breaks out of step and toward me across the field, but not looking in his direction or even directly ahead. Abruptly, the road curves and offers a lit sign—*"Bar-Restaurant-Sprecken-Sie-Deutsch"*—and I run toward it, cutting across an embankment, finding myself heading toward another bright, empty lobby. But the door to this place is unlocked, and I burst through it, panting.

"Hola." A girl appears, wiping her hands on her trousers.

"¿Habitación?" I answer, purely out of hope, because the sign says "Restaurant." It doesn't say "lodging."

"Sí." With minimal fuss—she doesn't ask for my passport or my credit card—she hands me a key, #1, and instructs me in a mix of English and Spanish to go back outside and to the left, where I'll find a staircase, at the top of which is a door marked with the number one.

There is a man out there, I could say, I *should* say, a man masturbating, but the potential difficulties of explaining this across language barriers, and the pantomimes that might be required, defeat me. "Right outside the door?" I ask.

"Yes," she says, and when I don't move she takes the key back. "Come. I show you."

At the top of the steps she inserts the key in the lock, opens the door, and then reaches inside to switch on the light. It's the only room they have, she tells me, the others aren't yet built, and there is no restaurant, just a bar.

"Thank you," I say. I listen to the noise of her shoes on the metal stair treads as she descends. The window reveals nothing; it's black outside.

Why does bathing, washing, folding, cleaning have such a profoundly calming effect? Is it that we reenact being cared for as children, helpless against dirt and disorder, when the only chaos we knew was this ultimately benign and reversible domestic chaos? For dinner I have cookies and water and dried fruit. I sit on the bed and chew, surveying my clothes as they hang from every knob and hook and sill, the radiator covered with wrung out garments, probably unsafe. Already the room smells of scorching cotton, but I can't stand being wet another day.

Three

Friday, March 26, 1999. 8:45 a.m. West of Disicabo.
I've gathered and folded my clothes and, pack on my
back, descended the long stairs outside my room. A
tersely efficient man, the father of the girl who showed
me to my room, stands behind the bar just off the lobby.
Without a word he sets my coffee on its shining surface,
the two of us reflected countless times in the mirrors that
panel this room—so many that to discern between the
actual and the image requires vigilance. I'd hate to be
drunk and looking for a bathroom in a bar like this one.
From one of the vending machines in the foyer I buy a little box of cookies and some *cacahuetes*—peanuts—vacuum
sealed in a foil and plastic wrap that is so tight I can see

the shape of the nuts within. I use my army knife to pierce it and air rushes in with a little gasp.

Regarded in the full light of morning—after a night's sleep—the previous evening's adventure seems comic, almost. And I'm much encouraged by how dry everything is: shoes and socks and long underwear. Outside, the sun shines, igniting all the wet foliage so that it gleams. The day begins in a pleasant solitude; I see no one ahead of me on the path, and no one follows. As I walk I realize that my insistence on leaving Palas de Rei yesterday had to do with the conviviality of the party of young men I met at Ligonde. They gave me an orange, made broken half-French conversation, called me brave and strong—all of which I enjoyed in the moment—but when they called, as we were leaving, "See you in Palas," I determined that this wouldn't happen. I didn't want to be drawn into a long, raucous dinner, the strain of conversation without fluency, and I didn't want to have to extricate myself from the inevitable invitation to eat together.

The road, a packed dirt path lined with poplars, recalls paintings by Corot or Sisley; it conveys peace and stillness, straight rather than meandering, without encouraging one to hurry. At 10:30 a.m. I make my first stop, at a tavern in Furelos, over which presides a can-tankerous old woman who, after demanding what I want—I say coffee and madeleines—continues a strident argument with another woman who gesticulates hysterically with a loaf a bread, a candle, and a dish of change that she slams down on the counter so that all the coins leap into the air. After a few minutes I stand, having given up on the coffee, and both women turn to me and yell something that begins with an *S* and which I take to mean "Sit!" Then the owner pours me coffee and the other woman—her sister? her friend?—slams a plate of cakes down next to my cup. I drink the coffee quickly, with both of them scowling at me, their arms folded across their stomachs. In apology for my interrupting them, I ask if I can buy one of the shell pendants that hang in a cluster behind the till. The woman who poured the coffee nods curtly at my pointing finger. She gets one down and writes the cost of it, plus the price of the coffee and cakes, on a slip of paper. Rather than remain any longer, I pay, pocket the cakes, and leave.

The walking is easy, flat and pretty without dramatic scenery, a path through land that seems untroubled. Every so often I see a little structure with a tiled roof and walls made of wood slats, a stone base, with a door at one end. Corncribs, I discover after stopping at one and teasing a husk out from between the slats, but so pretty and quaint that I'd mistaken them for tiny shrines, something with a symbolic rather than practical use.

What do I want of my arrival in Santiago? With fifty kilometers to go, or less, I feel sad and sore—tired enough that only more and more sugar can address my fatigue. As I told Colin during our last call, I feel that I am walking toward him, and I am: toward my home and my family. I wonder if I don't always feel that way about traveling—that it's an exercise in setting myself down far from home, and working my way back. This time it's more onerous, of course, and more literal. I walk each day a little closer to the conclusion of this journey.

I'm wearing the shell, a scallop with a red cross painted on the convex side. I carried it in my hand for an hour before slipping it over my head. Shells are available at many stops along the camino, but it's taken me six days to acquire this universal sign of the pilgrim to Santiago, and I try to understand my reluctance. Is it akin to my refusing to wear a crucifix, my dislike of outward signifiers? Yesterday, the men in Ligonde asked me where my shell was, and I shrugged, dismissing the question. A matter of pride, I think, of not wanting to identify myself with any group.

The most unexpected aspect of this walk has been the unprecedented peace of it. Wolves and exhibitionists and cross old women aside, the long periods of calm have instructed me in something I've had trouble understanding up until now: what genuine Zenlike detachment might be, a state of awareness untrammeled by passion. Not that I don't feel—I do, intensely—but I feel without being ensnared by the emotion, without the familiar spasms of longing. Paradoxically, I'm deep in my body while experiencing a bird's-eye view of myself on this road; it's acceptance, a sense that at last I am coming to accept those things I've struggled against. Not only am I happy in my life, but I feel strangely divested of events that have caused me unhappiness, like a vessel tipped out, washed, and at this moment in time, clean and empty. It's odd and it's pleasant. It feels good, restful. In contemplating this walk I pictured myself like Lear on the heath, wild weather and a chance to storm with it, far from witnesses, but it's a step-by-step trudging, stitch by stitch, and not at all dramatic, like a deep, deep pool with an unruffled surface.

The path has become a trench again, but this time it's lined with violets; they poke out from between the rocks.

2:45 p.m. Arzúa.
I call home from a gas station and the usual chaos tumbles through the line. Walker has just fallen down the

stairs; Sarah is tearful; Colin complains that the car's battery is dead again. I listen and try to console. All the problems are small, and comforting by virtue of their smallness; how easy to address such little woes, even from this distance. I hang up and sit on a low wall to consider my map. In three and a half hours I could reach Brea.

It's windy and overcast, green hills shadowed by clouds so dense they seem solid. So far west, so near to Santiago, the way markers are less frequent, and the air—can I be imagining this?—smells of the sea. It's a dark day, and dusk never arrives, blotted out by a wild and beautiful storm, the kind I would relish from beside a fire, indoors and listening to it blow around the eaves and splatter the windows. Outside, however, a poncho-tearing wind blows rain sideways into my eyes, slapping me in the face with the ripped poncho while soaking my trousers. The track dissolves into mud so liberally laced with cow dung that the smell burns the insides of my nostrils. Every so often I stumble into an invisible pot-hole, once down as far as my knee. On either side of the path are cows, huddled and unmoving, their flanks filthy, their tails dripping liquid excrement.

In spite of my map's encouraging drawing of a friendly clutch of buildings, Brea turns out to be a drip-ping gray intersection, without hotel or bar, and Salcidos, a few kilometers on, is also deserted, as if the populace had been washed away by the tide of dirty water coursing down the one street. Sitting on a stone wall, wet through to my underwear, I succumb to tears. The road has become so slick and slimy that twice I've lost my footing and fallen, wrenching my bad knee and injuring some new part of it. Now, going downhill is excruciating, so bad that I can only manage it by walking backward— an accidental discovery I make while turning helpless circles of woe. Not that it's easy, because I have to advance a few paces, then stop and turn around to see what lies in my path, but it is possible. After a few hills, I've refined the process into a step, step, step, pirouette-to-look, step, step, step, and so I go.

My last day of walking, tomorrow, will include many hills, which I will go up and then down, facing first forward and then backward, prompting a few stares, as if I were accomplishing an eccentric penance.

But it's not Saturday yet. It's still Friday night. Soaked and exhausted, I fall prey to the old fear of wolves when I notice, abruptly, that the sheep and the cows have all disappeared by six o'clock, gathered into the safety of barns. Walking west, the day's dim light fading at my back, I consider the possibility that I may be spending a night outside. I could find shelter, curl under my poncho with my head on my pack. But what about wolves? All around me, the gray landscape seems to tremble with their presence, every bent branch a slender leg, every wet glint a predatory eye. Would it be possible for me to be eaten by a wolf? As I walk west, still hoping for a hotel, a tavern from whose owner I might beg lodging, I keep asking the question. It seems so quaint, so medieval, so anti-postmodern. Too weird, even, to be ironic.

The muddy road sinks again into a trench, and I remind myself that I obsess when I'm tired, and that tomorrow will be an easy day: no more than twenty kilometers until I reach Santiago, where I have a reservation at a good hotel, a reservation guaranteed until six o'clock in the evening. If I got to the holy city by three or four, I'd have time to buy clothes that I could wear to Mass on Sunday, Palm Sunday. Unaccountably, the idea of Mass in a cathedral is a catalyst for tears; perhaps it's the idea of shelter, the smell of the incense, candle flames.

Do I walk for some time with my eyes half-closed against the rain, my face averted from the wind? When I pause to readjust my pack and poncho, square my shoulders and look ahead of me, I see a cluster of yellow lights and, a few steps farther on, an illuminated sign: *"Hotel-Restaurant O'Pino,"* a vision so unexpected that I wonder for a moment if I've conjured it. But it doesn't twinkle or tremble like a mirage, and neither does it fade. And Señor Ramón Carril Rial, who presents his business card to me as I step inside the door to his inn, appears quite real and solid, if diminutive. He looks at me, dripping on his clean floor. "¿Habitación?" he asks. "¿Con baño?"

I nod, "Sí. Gracias. Gracias."

He holds out a key and points, a little sadly it seems, across his clean lobby to a lit corridor. I stand without moving. Should I take off my poncho, or will that precipitate an even larger cascade of dirty water?

"Agua cálida," Señor Ramón says, as if to spur me on, and so I squelch off, poncho still in place.

Once I'm in the bathtub, a long one filled with water as hot as I can stand, filled to the point that even a deep breath causes it to overflow, it's only the prospect of missing dinner that tempts me out. When I look at myself in the mirror, I see a distinct line across my torso: Above it the skin is white, below, where my body has been submerged in hot water, red. Steam rises off my legs and flanks. Rather than drain the tub, I sort my clothes into piles of almost clean, merely grimy, and filthy, and dump the latter into the water, watching them sink slowly.

In the dining room, I eat alone, served by Señor Ramón, who doesn't offer me a menu with a choice of entrées, but brings me typical pilgrim fare: a bowl of thick bean soup, a basket of bread, a plate of meat and potatoes, a carafe of red wine. Inside my clothes, my one dry shirt tucked into my damp and dirty trousers—no underwear because all of it was sopped—I feel as if I'm on fire, flushed with food and wine and dry heat. Across the empty room I see myself reflected in the wet black windowpanes. As usual, I'm surprised by my size; I'm smaller than I think of myself as being, smaller and more intent.

The phone in my room rings while I'm wringing out the clothes I left soaking. Señor Ramón wants to know when I plan on leaving, and I realize I haven't paid for anything, neither room nor dinner, and, perhaps out of consideration for my disheveled and exhausted state, he never requested any passport or credit card when I arrived.

"Tomorrow," I say. *"Mañana. ¿Al desayuno?"* At breakfast, I think I've suggested.

"Sí, sí," he answers, sounding satisfied, and he's waiting for me when I emerge the next morning, dressed and packed, if not exactly dry.

Saturday, March 27, 1999. 8:00 a.m. West of Arzúa.
Outside it's still raining, and I turn my back on the windows to eat what Señor Ramón brings to the bar: freshly

baked bread, still hot, with honey, a pot of coffee and a pitcher of boiled milk. Like dinner, it tastes so good that I'm almost tearful as I thank him. "No," he says, "too much," and he pushes back my extravagant tip, looking at my ragged trousers and ruined shoes. The bill for everything—dinner, room, breakfast—is 5,110 pesetas, not even thirty-five dollars.

Everything hurts, my knee especially, but this is the last day, this is the day I will arrive in Santiago and, as if taking its cue from my perfect breakfast and bright mood, the rain stops as I set out. Clouds, dark and gorgeous, purple rimmed with silver, part theatrically to reveal the sun, which in its turn shines on a world that is freshly washed and sparkling. By 10:30 a.m. I'm sitting on a bridge over the River Lavacolla, meaning "wash your collar"—a last chance to spruce up before arrival in the holy city, a mere eleven kilometers away. Sun shines among the moss-covered tree trunks in thick columns of stunning greeny gold, the like of which I've never seen in real life, only in the hyperreal, overwrought, and intensely colored emotion of a Pre-Raphaelite painting. All of nature hums with numinous significance.

Just west of the bridge, I walk past a farm, and a man beckons to me. "Hey," he calls, standing on the bottom rung of a split-rail fence. "Come, señora, see." In his yard is a cow, pale and beautiful, an enchanted beast with eyelashes as long as my fingers, and thrusting at her udder are two calves, prettier than any I've seen before. The farmer smiles as I look. *"¿Bonita?"* he asks, and I agree.

"¡Sí! Sí! Muy bonita!"

I almost want to clap, but I stand still, my hands folded, and watch as they suckle. The calves are the most wonderful color, like caramel or toffee, a perfect sweet creamy beige that sets off a little avalanche of associations: the Cromwell toffee my grandfather kept in his desk drawer, and which, after he died, melted and wept out of the box, gluing together all his papers, bills, and tax receipts with layers of sweet candy. And aren't they, too, the color of my mother's toffee, those pans of it she cooked and cooled and topped with a layer of dark chocolate? She cut the sweet expanse with a knife, arranged the neat squares on a plate, two bites a piece. On the sly I chewed them into syrup and spat them down sink drains, every once in a while miscalculating and having to swallow, because someone caught me in the hall and asked a question. But mostly I got away with the crime, a perversion of having my cake and eating it, my refusal to swallow my mother's labor, her talent, her gift. I look up at the farmer's smile, still intact, as he watches his animals.

My entrance to the city is marked by a sudden dramatic downpour, rain strikes the ground hard enough to bounce as I walks through a forest of eucalyptus—a species of tree that seems not just unlikely here, but impossible. Are they not native to Australia? Why introduce them here, in the midst of lush European forests? As I walk, I keep picking up the long leaves and crushing them under my nose to release their distinctive, unmistakable smell. The Santiago airport must be nearby: I can't see it, but I can hear planes as they taxi and take off, and the noise adds a surreal, even apocalyptic dimension to the already weird atmosphere. The day is one of those in which sun competes with rain and wind. Ominous clouds scud overhead, blotting out the light for brief, disorienting intervals. The wind picks up my poncho and slaps me in the face, over and over with a kind of determination and insult, as if it were chastising me. I keep it on for as long as I can stand it—underneath I am carrying unwrapped bread—but after one particularly wet and stinging assault I succumb to temper and, seeing a garbage can, tear it off and rip it vengefully in half before thrusting it among discarded greasy food wrappers. I have never thrown any object away with greater delight.

It takes time to penetrate the disappointing outskirts of Santiago, but the old city is graceful and lovely,
its streets narrow and twisting and cobbled, with bright
shop windows revealing all sorts of temptations: choco-
lates, toys, wine, necklaces, books. Eager as I am to reach
the cathedral, I linger at every corner; I see few things
that I don't imagine myself buying.

I reach the stairs to the cathedral door at 2:30 p.m.,
and pause before I climb them. My knees are shaking
with something like fatigue, but also, I suspect, appre-
hension. Isn't my destination guaranteed to disappoint
me, to make me feel a fool? After all, I've seen Europe's
grandest churches: sat among the gargoyles on the roof
of Notre-Dame; dizzied my eyes with St. Peter's *bal-
dacchino;* happened, one gray afternoon, into Chartres,
having taken a detour that delivered me to the cathedral
just as someone was rehearsing on the pipe organ, belch-
ing clouds of Bach so violently sublime that they para-
lyzed. A crowd of us were held captive in the nave, missing trains and forgetting tour buses. So what can I find
here, after so long a walk?

The Pórtico de la Gloria, a grand arched entrance
wreathed with figures carved of stone, forbids as thoroughly as it beckons. Ranged around the door a celestial
orchestra plays lutes, lyres, violins, the musicians' stone
faces tipped heavenward in blind ecstasy, their eyes

closed, their hands frozen mid-note, their beards curled into stone ringlets as stylized and impossible as treble clefs. I pass beneath them, thinking less of God than of man, of woman, of Lot's wife, who haunts my every encounter with religious statuary, flesh made into example. How unfair to be punished for looking back, punished for refusing to relinquish affection, memory, horror: the very attributes that make us human.

One in a long queue of grubby, limping pilgrims, I file past the sepulcher of James, kiss the saint's shell, and receive the anointing touch of a silent priest. Feeling the press of bodies on either side, I look up for the relief of a high ceiling, balm to the claustrophobic, but above me the cathedral dome is decorated with a terrifying Ojo de Dios, a great staring human eye painted with a thick paternal brow. God watches, his pupil, the size of a platter, ringed with golden brown, his lids spiked with lashes and deeply shadowed. Here is an eye that never closes. Alone, in the absence of a mate, it looks aghast and visionary.

I flee the cold sanctuary for the gift shop, where, relieved by the possibility of a simple transaction, I buy a few pious trinkets. Then I am back out in the wet day, hungry and cold. A map from the tourist office reveals that the hotel where I am to stay the night is not nearly as central as I'd hoped, but my reservation is guaranteed—I have the confirmation in my pack—and on the eve of Palm Sunday, during a holy year, I am happy to have any room, on any street. I buy a half kilo of strawberries from a vendor on a street corner, and begin my damp climb up the narrow slippery cobbles. A good dinner, I think, an amazing dinner, as I pass one after another door decorated with Diners Club and American Express stickers, framed menus offering four courses before dessert.

But when the hour to dress for dinner arrives, I am in bed drinking cheap scotch from the minibar and watching CNN. It's so windy outside that each gust howls like the wolves that have preoccupied me so often at this hour, and how can I get up, how can I put on my wet shoes and damp dirty trousers? Instead I fall asleep, helpless to resist the combined warmth of bed and scotch. When I wake, at eight, the same tape of the same distant war in Bosnia is being broadcast, with commentary by the same anchorwoman. Having spent days living in real time—not writing time or brain time or screen time, but footstep time, time measured by daylight, hunger, the body—I've abruptly, in the space of an afternoon, lost touch with all that. Or have I?

I turn off the television and find my reflection in the mirror over the dresser. My usually pale cheeks are flaming red, an effect of the scotch, no doubt, as well as windburn, but together with my extraordinarily tangled hair, they make me look younger, almost like a child. I think of the last hill, the vision of the cathedral's bell tower rising over the city, the goal in reach. Was that the arrival? The center of Santiago struck me with the same melancholy as that of every historic city center: lovely, graceful, and sad. These places we guard so carefully and proudly against time—they always seem small and vulnerable, less triumphant than compromised. Unbidden, the little calves return, and with them the plate of my mother's candy.

I want to go to sleep, trapped as I am in this unobjectionable room, unable to dress in my cold clothes, unable to walk a step that isn't required. I want to sleep and wake at six, allowing me four hours of Palm Sunday, Communion under the eye of God, before I have to pack and make my plane. And, unexpectedly, I do.

Sunday, March 28, 1999. 6:00 a.m. Santiago.
Having woken at the hour I intend, I take a long hot bath and by 7:30 am dressed and sitting at a small table in the dining room. Unlimited café con leche, a basket of hot rolls, muesli and yogurt and fruit: I eat and go on eating, then walk, without my pack, to attend Mass in the cathedral, legs stiff and back light.

During the service it's my misfortune to sit next to a nun who is offended by my grubby and unfeminine attire, so much so that she cannot bring herself to look at me, not even when the congregants are directed by the priest to offer one another a sign of peace. But the little sting is assuaged by the Mass's climax: the lighting of the Botafumeiro. Somehow, I walked all this way not knowing enough to expect it, the cathedral's famed silver censer, so big that it requires eight priests to carry it to the altar. Dressed in red robes, they process from a side chapel, bearing the censer on a thick, polished pole, padded at each end to protect their shoulders. The priests set the censer before the altar, remove its top, and fill the great bowl with incense, which they ignite before hurriedly replacing the top. The black mechanism hanging under the dome's painted eye is revealed as a winch, from which a rope as thick as a man's arm dangles; one end of the rope is fixed, by means of a gargantuan knot, to the Botafumeiro, the other end is attached to eight smaller ropes, one for each priest.

Smoke pours from the many perforations in the lid of the censer, obscuring its burnished sides, its decorative shell and crucifix motifs. The priests take and pull their ropes, and it ascends. With the swift economy of long practice, the robed figures pull and release, pull and release, setting the huge burning orb into an arc of motion that swings through the cathedral's transept, back and forth, wider and wider, trailing smoke and perfume until high over the congregation's heads it looks like a captured comet: the polished head trails flames, a long tail of smoke, and twinkling orange sparks. A choking sweet cloud envelops its audience. Spectacular and so, so beautiful! Everyone in the church is standing, face tipped up, eyes following the great hypnotic pendulum as it swings as much as a hundred feet back and forth. How wonderful and perfect to be taken by surprise by it.

I spill with the crowd out of the cathedral and down the steps, throat burning and eyes watering. Disoriented, elated, it takes me a moment to recognize the four young men who beckon from the plaza, calling "¡Hola!" and "Hey" and "Señora," and waving their stamped pilgrim passports. It's the group of bicyclists I met in Ligonde, with whom I drank bad coffee while we avoided the wind and rain.

"When did you get here?" one asks in French.

"*Hier,*" I say. Yesterday.

"Where is your certificate?"

I shrug, and the one who gave me the orange laughs. "Her," he says, "she doesn't need one." We laugh at the distance I walked since our meeting. Apparently I beat them by a day.

As I walk back to the hotel, back to my pack and the car reserved to take me to the airport, a woman presses an olive branch in my hand. *"Paz,"* she says, and then in English. "Peace."

What will be left? I ask myself as my flight to London departs from the local airport. Through the airplane's window the city of Santiago shrinks, recedes. What will I remember? I'm happy not to have brought a camera, grateful to have a reason to hold this image of light in my memory: a path worn down into the earth, woods on either side and shafts of gold coming through the tree trunks. Don't let me forget, I ask. Please make me remember.

In my lap I make a list:

I walked 283 kilometers in seven days.

I limped 100 of those kilometers.

I ended each day in tears.

I fell twice, once on the first day and once on the last.

I went to Mass twice.

I had sun every day and rain for four days.

I was barked at every day.

I worried about wolves.

I kissed a stone cross, and I stole some holy oil, received stamps and stamped myself.

I thought of Colin, Sarah, Walker, my mother and my father, my grandparents and my friends—books I've written and those I hope to write. The baby I want to have, not yet even the proverbial twinkle, and yet she exists, exists as desire.

What do I know that my children haven't taught me? Though it's not something I can imagine, three years hence I'll return to this road with my older daughter, and through her eyes see myself. It will require days of walking in step for Sarah to show me that grace humbles as often as it exalts, and always arrives in an unexpected form. This time I traveled in a fever, as if I believed I had wings; the next walk will be this journey's necessary complement, showing me my feet of clay.

In London, a canceled flight affords me the use of the first-class lounge—the airline's apology for causing me inconvenience—and I discover with delight that the lounge includes not only food and drink but a suite of showers and dressing rooms, endless hot water and unlimited towels and bottles of shampoo, conditioner, lotion.

Glowing and clean under my grubby clothes, I watch CNN while drinking a glass of red wine, hardly caring that enough time has passed that I'm watching a second replay of a videotaped interview with the widow of a Bosnian freedom fighter. The woman, who had not seen her husband for two years before his death, stressed how lucky she was to have married such a generous man, a supportive and honorable man. "No one can take that from me," she says. "It is mine." Listening to this for the third time, I don't feel my usual irritation with CNN's endless repetition of tape. Instead it bursts upon me like a revelation. Many times Colin and I have observed my preoccupation with the past, in contrast with his plans for the future, its potential and its freedom.

What hope the future holds. The past has none of these, but, as this stranger from a strange land has just revealed: The past is mine. No one can take it from me. Suddenly all those whom I think of as lost—my mother and father, my grandmother and grandfather—seem equally found. How much I hold within myself, enough that I need never be bereft. Sitting in the lounge, my shoes so filthy they draw stares from the soigné first-class crowd, I close my eyes and see everyone I love, just as I did on the road, luminous and exalted and mine.

Kathryn Harrison is the author of five novels, *Thicker Than Water, Exposure, Poison, The Binding Chair,* and *The Seal Wife;* three memoirs, *The Kiss, Seeking Rapture,* and *Breakwater* (2004); and a biography, *Saint Thérèse of Lisieux.* She is married to the novelist Colin Harrison, with whom she has three children.

This book is set in Garamond 3, designed by
Morris Fuller Benton and Thomas Maitland
Cleland in the 1930s, and Monotype Grotesque,
both released digitally by Adobe.

Printed by R. R. Donnelley and Sons on
Gladfelter 60-pound Thor Offset smooth
white antique paper.

Dust jacket printed by Miken Companies.
Color separation by Quad Graphics.

Three-piece case of Ecological Fiber cafe side
panels with Sierra black book cloth as the spine
fabric. Stamped in Lustrofoil metallic silver.

I profited? Nothing, and not at all. In fact, didn't it obscure what I wanted: to know each of us, mother, father, grandmother, grandfather, and myself. Wasn't it just a great fortress of defenses, erected against the truth that, in spite of our failings, our insurmountable failings, we had loved one another?

Before me, the beckoning, sinister edifice collapses, vanishes over the green, and in its place I see my family bleeding light: They are that beautiful. My grandfather is kneeling in his garden. My grandmother, flushed and animated, is telling a story. My mother is dressing for a date, patting that last strand of hair into place. My father holds a camera in his hands. And not just the past but the present comes crowding in, my husband with his broad back, stacking stones to make a wall—how I wish he were beside me to see all the ancient dry walls—my children laughing, and friends—amazing friends, the profound mystery of friendship: love outside of lust or blood.

Penance, walking on blisters, counting up ever more coins of virtue and suffering with which to pay my way—how much easier this is for me to accept than the notion that I deserve, and can purchase, nothing of all that I have.

"*¿Qué pasa?*"

"A Santiago."

"*¿Solita?!*"

"Sí."

"*¡Ay yi!*"

It's almost as if I have a new name, Solita, and all the old women want to know it. The men stare, hands hanging at their sides, but the women, true crones with their heads covered with kerchiefs, lay down whatever is in their hands, a pail, a bundle of sticks, the handle of a hoe, and demand what it is that I'm doing. ¿Qué pasa?

At seven o'clock—five kilometers until I reach Sarria, where I will spend the night—what I'm doing is scrambling up the side of a rock to avoid being swept along with a herd of cows hurried homeward by a man and his dog. Once they pass, I sit for a while, trying to make out the distance to Sarria, the time it will take for me to reach the town, which, mirage-like, beckons and eludes.

The problem, I discover as I walk more and more slowly, is that Sarria is not a small town but a little city. I draw closer; it claims a wider and wider piece of the horizon, but remains in the distance. The road is only intermittently paved, and punctuated by warnings, "*¡Perro peligroso!*" accompanied by pictures of slavering dogs with fangs. The chained dogs lie in the dust, their eyes slit, assessing. Only one considers me worthy of a bark; the rest just watch as I limp toward town. Early spring twilight seems endless. The sun set hours ago, and yet it isn't dark at eight, just a cool blue gray, pocked by the yellow lights of Sarria.

Abruptly, the walk is awful. Not only am I lame, limping to favor my right knee, but I'm so tired I feel faint and nauseated. Every few hundred yards I stop and, at the prospect of standing and going on, consider hitchhiking to the nearest hotel. But it seems impossible to flag down a driver and successfully pantomime what I want. I'm so dulled by exhaustion that I can't imagine doing anything except struggling to my feet, lifting the pack, and trudging forward to the lights. Scenery has given way to an attenuated suburbia, a dirt road lined by a string of graceless houses made of concrete and stucco, with pens of sheep in the back and debris—old plastic sacks and car parts—spread in the front. Every so often I see one of the more familiar old houses built of stone, complete with an old woman in front, toothless and staring. One spits something into her withered palm and considers it in the half light.

Since my lunch of coffee and madeleines, I've been fantasizing about elaborate dinners, but, when I at last reach Sarria's main street and see a fruit store, I stop and buy a bag of clementines and peel them as I walk, not bothering to separate the segments but eating whole halves of the sweet little oranges. When I stop at the Hotel Londres, the first lodging I see, the woman behind the desk looks at my grimy, sticky, juice-stained fingers with disapproval. "¿Solita?" she inquires, and I nod. I try not to cry when she points to the staircase that separates me from my room, which turns out to be a claustrophobic little hole, windowless, with walls, floor, and ceiling covered in marble patterned plastic tile. I wash my face in the stained sink and re-layer my shirts so that the less dirty one is on top, but I don't take off my trousers, because that would require taking off my shoes, and I don't want to see my feet until after I've had at least one glass of wine.

From the sidewalk in front of the Hotel Londres I look up and down the street, measuring steps to the two restaurants in sight. At the closer one, I order what I think will be an omelet but seems, on inspection, to be tuna fish held together by a web of cooked egg, the sight of which provokes a startling and visceral memory of a woman—her name was Billie Amons—who used to clean my grandmother's house in Los Angeles. Billie came once a week, on Wednesdays, and was a large black woman who fascinated and impressed me for all the ways she differed from my mother and my grandmother. She made lunch for herself from whatever leftovers she found in our refrigerator, dumping containers indiscriminately into a skillet and frying eggs around it all to hold the ingredients together. She made lunch for me, too, crustless butter sandwiches cut in fourths, and we sat together in the breakfast nook, I on the cracked red vinyl banquette and she in a chrome-legged kitchen chair. Without meaning to, I often made Billie laugh, and when she did I could see a gold tooth in the back of her mouth. Her skin shined as if polished, and she smelled like lemons. For my sixth birthday she gave me a pair of flannel pajamas, printed all over with red cabbage roses, pajamas that were "impossible" according to my mother. Many times I had to retrieve them from the garbage can.

A glass of red wine quickens the memory into something like grief; or perhaps, like a small child, I am weeping because I am tired. The waiter wrings his hands and pours more wine into my glass as I try to spare both of us further embarrassment by writing in my journal.

Wednesday, March 24, 1999. 8:00 a.m. Sarria.
I wake after ten hours sleep, my sore knee better but not cured by the rest. Tiger Balm has left a stain on the bed's bottom sheet, an ochre outline of my bent right knee,

and I study it. I must have been tired enough to sleep on my side without moving, without disturbing the blankets, which remain tightly tucked at the foot of the bed.

Two cafés con leche, two madeleines, half a Power Bar, and three clementines later, I'm still waiting for the *farmacia* across the street to open. The hotel bar is an offensive place, already filled, at nine o'clock in the morning, with people drinking and smoking, but I'm not moving until I get some Advil. Who are these men who begin the day with cigarettes and shot glasses? They regard me, and I them, with curiosity.

The farmacias of Spain are like tiny shrines, so different from America's vast and overwhelming Rite Aids and Kmarts, their endless aisles of too many products: how to choose among so many toothpastes and shampoos? On some occasions I'm defeated by the surfeit of options and leave without buying anything. But the stores I encounter along the camino are small, wares displayed as though they have real value. Like icons they sit on doilies. A cabinet contains two hair products from which to choose, one brand of sunscreen, hand lotion, cotton swabs, a nameless dentifrice—"toothpaste" seems too modern a word for the small blue tube—and a dozen toothbrushes, without cartoon characters or Barbie monogrammed onto their handles. A single Rite Aid could fully stock a hundred of these little farmacias.

Behind a glass display counter, its shelves holding a few black plastic combs and single disposable razors, is the saleslady, wearing a navy blue cardigan and eyeglasses on a chain. After a series of mispronunciations and pantomimes, I write one word on a page from my journal—ibuprofen—and she nods. From a drawer behind her, she withdraws a bottle of sixteen tablets.

On the way out of town I make two stops, first at a market to buy food, and second at the Convento de Mercaderios church, where I watch a priest instruct children in Holy Week ritual. The sanctuary is lovely and peaceful, the class of eight- or ten-year-olds solemn. There is some symmetry here: my sitting with a bundle of food in my lap, watching children in their attempt to understand the sacred. How far backward into my own life would I have to walk before I might begin to understand my hunger and what could satisfy it? Through the plastic film of the grocery bag I touch what I've bought at the market: water, half a baguette, a container of yogurt, an apple. I wanted chocolate, weighed a bar in my hands, considered it, and then replaced it on the shelf. How many centuries has it been that the church has equated the sacrifice of the body's demands, its pleasures, with the growth of the spirit?

By eleven o'clock I've eaten the apple and a few inches of the baguette. Just beyond the town of Barbadelo, a man is burning scrub to clear a patch of land. Wind carries ash far from his fire, and I watch the black fragments drift across the blue sky, a few falling on the path before me. Roosters crow; I've been hearing them all morning. And the way is peppered with old women, ubiquitous and emblematic old women moving slowly among the oak trees, the green fields. It seems as if the process of aging has stripped away whatever modernity they might have once possessed, that the present with its cars and computers has peeled off these women like a second skin, to reveal crones the same as those pictured in books of fairy tales. Wearing aprons and head scarves, bearing baskets or bundles, they have a witchy look, as if they might produce poisoned apples from under their cloaks.

The fields are enclosed by slate walls called *chantos,* a vestige of Galicia's Celtic past. A group of students passes, chattering, and I realize that I'm walking slowly today, and stopping more often. I sit on one of the walls to eat my yogurt and four turkeys appear, walking abreast, like the students, but in silence. They pump their heads purposefully, and when I make a gobbling